Timothy Keller

Romans 1-7

The Gift of God

● 7-Session Bible Study

Romans For You

These studies are adapted from *Romans 1–7 For You*. If you are reading *Romans 1–7 For You* alongside this Good Book Guide, here is how the studies in this booklet link to the chapters of *Romans 1–7 For You*:

Study 1 > Ch 1
Study 2 > Ch 2-4
Study 3 > Ch 5-6
Study 4 > Ch 7

Study 5 > Ch 8-9
Study 6 > Ch 10-11
Study 7 > Ch 12

Find out more about *Romans 1–7 For You* at:
www.thegoodbook.com/for-you

Romans 1–7: The Gift of God
A Good Book Guide
© Timothy Keller/The Good Book Company, 2014.
This edition printed 2025.

Published by The Good Book Company

thegoodbook.com | thegoodbook.co.uk
thegoodbook.com.au | thegoodbook.co.nz

Unless indicated, all Scripture references are taken from the Holy Bible, New International Version. Copyright © 1973, 1978, 1984 by the International Bible Society. Used by permission.

Timothy Keller has asserted his right under the Copyright, Designs and Patents Act 1988 to be identified as author of this work.

All rights reserved. Except as may be permitted by the Copyright Act, no part of this publication may be reproduced in any form or by any means without prior permission from the publisher.

A CIP catalogue record for this book is available from the British Library.

Design by André Parker and Drew McCall

ISBN: 9781802541908 | JOB-008230 | Printed in India

Contents

Introduction ... 4
Why Study Romans 1–7? ... 5

1. Introducing Righteousness ... 7
   Romans 1:1-17

2. Why Everyone Needs the Gospel ... 13
   Romans 1:18 – 2:29

3. How to Be Right with God ... 19
   Romans 3

4. What Abraham and David Discovered ... 27
   Romans 4

5. Enjoying Justification ... 33
   Romans 5

6. Why Christians Obey God ... 39
   Romans 6:1 – 7:6

7. Warfare Within ... 47
   Romans 7:7-25

Leader's Guide ... 53

# Introduction

One of the Bible writers described God's word as "a lamp for my feet, a light on my path" (Psalm 119:105, NIV). God gave us the Bible to tell us about who he is and what he wants for us. He speaks through it by his Spirit and lights our way through life.

That means that we need to look carefully at the Bible and uncover its meaning—but we also need to apply what we've discovered to our lives.

Good Book Guides are designed to help you do just that. The sessions in this book are interactive and easy to lead. They're perfect for use in groups or for personal study.

Let's take a look at what is included in each session.

Talkabout: Every session starts with an ice-breaker question, designed to get people talking around a subject that links to the Bible study.

Investigate: These questions help you explore what the passage is about.

Apply: These questions are designed to get you thinking practically: what does this Bible teaching mean for you and your church?

Explore More: These optional sections help you to go deeper or to explore another part of the Bible which connects with the main passage.

Getting Personal: These sections are a chance for personal reflection. Some groups may feel comfortable discussing these, but you may prefer to look at them quietly as individuals instead—or leave them out.

Pray: Here, you're invited to pray in the light of the truths and challenges you've seen in the study.

Each session is also designed to be easily split into two! Watch out for the **Apply** section that comes halfway through, and stop there if you haven't got time to do the whole thing in one go.

In the back of the book, you'll find a **Leader's Guide**, which provides helpful notes on every question, along with everything else that group leaders need in order to facilitate a great session and help the group uncover the riches of God's light-giving word.

Why Study Romans 1 - 7?

Everyone wants to be all right—to be in right standing, or "righteous."

We want to be right in the eyes of the law of our land—so we stay out of trouble. We want to be righteous in the eyes of those we respect and those we live among—so we act, speak, and dress in ways which are expected and acceptable. We want to be righteous in the eyes of our loved ones—so we seek, and then seek to keep, a partner, or partners. We want to be righteous in the eyes of those we work with—so we work hard, and work long.

But there is another, far better righteousness—the righteousness that Paul's letter to the church in Rome is all about. It is a righteousness which we all need, which all those other righteousnesses are pointers to, which changes and liberates every aspect of our lives.

It is to be right with God—to enjoy knowing him now, and to be able to look forward to enjoying knowing him forever. And this is a righteousness which, the apostle Paul told these Christians living in the capital of the known world, no one can earn or maintain themselves. No amount of effort or achievement can secure it.

Paul wanted them and us to realize something of eternal importance and life-changing liberation: that God *gives* people a right relationship with him. "The *gift of God*," he told them," is eternal life in Christ Jesus our Lord" (Romans 6:23).

In these seven studies, you'll see Paul teaching us about this gift of being right with God. You'll discover why, however religious we may be, we are not naturally righteous; how it is that, in Christ, God makes the unrighteous righteous; and what being righteous means for our future and our present.

And, as you unwrap this gift of God—as Paul challenges, teaches, and thrills you—you'll find that your lives, identities, and perspectives are transformed.

Carl Laferton
Editor

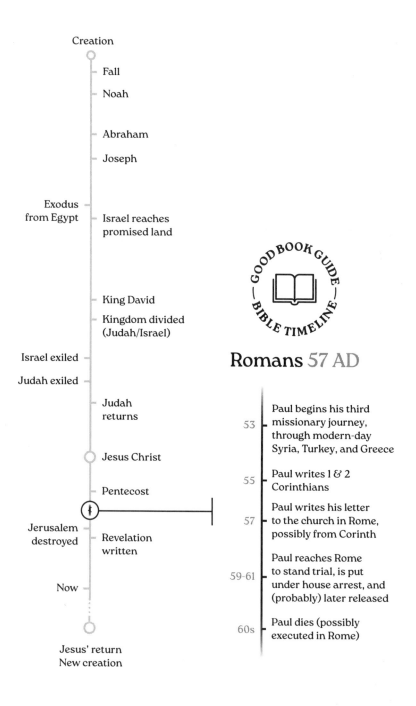

1

Introducing Righteousness

Romans 1:1-17

Talkabout

1. How would you sum up the message of Christianity in one sentence?

Investigate

📖 **Read Romans 1:1-13**

> **DICTIONARY**
>
> **Apostle** (v 1): a man who had seen the risen Jesus and was chosen by him to teach his word.
> **Gospel** (v 1): announcement (often of good news).
> **Holiness** (v 4): set-apart-ness.
> **Grace** (v 5): unmerited favor.
> **Saints** (v 7): holy people.

2. How did Paul view himself and his life (v 1, 5)?

3. What do the first six verses tell us about "the gospel"?

4. What does true faith result in (v 5)?

- Why is this, do you think?

5. Who is Paul writing to (v 7)? How does he describe them?

- How is he praying for them (v 8-10)?

- Why does he want to visit them (v 11-13)?

Apply

6. How can we mutually encourage each other as Christians today?

Getting Personal | OPTIONAL

God has declared that Jesus is his Son, raised with power to rule in power; and under his rule, we enjoy grace from and peace with him. When we spend time with other believers, we are spending time with those who say "This is true" and "This is wonderful" to that declaration.

How does this both encourage and challenge your attitude to your church services?

How are you relying on other Christians' gifts, and serving them with yours? Do you need to do more of one or the other (or both)?

Investigate

📖 **Read Romans 1:14-17**

> **DICTIONARY**
>
> **Obligated** or **bound** (v 14): in debt.
> **Greeks** (v 14): the people who had produced the wisest philosophers.
> **Ashamed** (v 16): the Greek word also means "offended."
>
> **Righteousness** (v 17): right standing with God.
> **From God** or **of God** (v 17): this phrase can be translated either way.

7. How does Paul feel about the gospel (v 15)? How does he not feel (v 16)?

- Why might people have a view of the gospel that is opposite from Paul's view?

8. Why is Paul *not* ashamed (v 14, 16)?

9. Put Paul's nutshell summary of the Christian message from verse 17a into your own words.

Explore More | OPTIONAL

- Who is the gospel for (v 14, 16)? Why does Paul underline this truth, do you think?
- Who does the gospel save (v 16-17)?
- What happens if we forget…
    - the unlimited nature of the gospel message?
    - that people are not saved if they do not believe that message?
- Which are you more likely to forget?

10. What does the end of verse 17 remind us about the Christian life?

Apply

11. What have verses 14-17 taught us about…
    - the debt of the gospel?

    - the power of the gospel?

    - the content of the gospel?

    - Why would forgetting any of these lead us to keep quiet about the gospel?

12. In what ways can we forget that "the righteous will live by faith" in the gospel?

Getting Personal | OPTIONAL

The gospel will always cause offense. So we will always be tempted to be ashamed of it. And the opposite of being ashamed is not willingness; it is eagerness (v 15).

Think of a time in your life when you have been eager to share the gospel. Why were you so eager?

When are you ashamed of the gospel? How will you remember verses 16-17 next time you are in that situation, and what difference will that make?

Pray

Thank God…

- *for your church, and how it encourages you in your faith and obedience.*
- *for the truth that God has both shown and offered his righteousness in the gospel.*
- *that righteousness is always about faith, not performance.*

Ask God…

- *to give you boldness in sharing the gospel, and to show you if or when you are ashamed.*

2

Why Everyone Needs the Gospel

Romans 1:18 – 2:29

The Story So Far...

Paul is writing to the Roman church about the gospel: the news that God's righteousness has been revealed by, and can be received from, Jesus.

Talkabout

1. If you asked 100 people, "What is wrong with the world?" what answers would you get?

- If you asked those people, "What would fix what is wrong?" what answers would you get?

Investigate

📖 **Read Romans 1:18-32**

DICTIONARY

Wrath (v 18): deserved, settled anger.
Futile (v 21): useless.
Perversion (v 27): corruption; something that is wrong.

Depraved (v 28): wicked, morally corrupt.
Malice (v 29): planning to hurt or do evil to someone.

---

2. What do verses 18-21 tell us about God's wrath?

3. Paul is talking about humans who reject the knowledge and worship of God. What does he say always happens to people who do this (v 22-25)?

4. What are some of the consequences of not wanting to know God (v 21, 26-32)?

Apply

5. How do we see the reality of God's present wrath in the world around us?

6. Do you think your church community is less prone to this truth-suppression and idol-worship than the surrounding culture? Why do you think this?

Getting Personal | OPTIONAL

The main problem of our heart is not so much our desire for bad things, but our over-desire for good things—our turning of created, good things into gods, objects of our worship and service.

What are the three created things you are most tempted to treat as gods, believing that they can fulfill and satisfy you?

What would it look like for you to see those things rightly, as things made by God? What would change if you enjoyed them in ways which worshiped and thanked God?

Investigate

📖 **Read Romans 2:1-29**

DICTIONARY

Repentance (v 4): changing your mind to accept God as King and Savior.
Law (v 12): God's standards, revealed in his word.
Gentiles (v 14): all people who aren't Jews.

Embodiment (v 20): visible form; best example.
Abhor (v 22): hate.
Circumcision (v 25) and **circumcised** (v 26): the way God told his people to show they were members of his people. (See Genesis 17.)

---

7. What kind of person is Paul addressing in verses 1-3? (Verse 17 may help.)

- What point is he making to them?

- What does he warn them of (v 4-5)?

Getting Personal | OPTIONAL

"Do you think you will escape God's judgment" because you avoid sins that others commit (v 3)?

God will use our own standards—the judgments we made with our own mouths—as the standards by which we are judged. Our behavior and our thoughts will be judged against how we thought and said others should live.

What are the places in which you are most likely to judge others and/or look down on them for doing things that you, in one way or another, do or think yourself?

Explore More | OPTIONAL

God "will give each person according to what he has done" (v 6). Judgment will be on the basis of works. Has Paul changed his mind since Romans 1:16-17, where he said right standing with God is given by him, received by us by faith, and never earned?

Read Psalm 62

This is the psalm Paul is quoting from. David, the writer, is contrasting two groups of people.

- What is the first group like (v 3-4)? What have they "done" in terms of how they relate to God?
- What have the second group "done" (v 1, 7)?
- So what does David mean in verse 12, when he says each group will be rewarded "according to what [they have] done"?

- How does this help us understand Paul in Romans 2:6-11?

In Psalm 62:9-10, we see that saving faith does show itself in actions: "the obedience that comes from faith" (Romans 1:5). In this sense good works, while not adding to faith in saving someone, do show that they have saving faith. They are the outward sign of the internal faith.

- What is the challenge here for professing Christians?

Paul says that everyone who doesn't know the law of God will "perish apart from the law," and those who do know it will "be judged by the law" (v 12).

8. How does he show that there is no defense before God for...
   - unreligious people (v 13-16)?

   - religious people (v 17-27)?

9. What is the only thing that really matters (v 28-29)?

   - What does this kind of heart result in, both negatively and positively (end of verse 29)? Why, do you think?

Apply

10. How would we know if we were the "you" Paul is addressing in chapter 2?

11. If someone asked you, "What is wrong with the world?" what answer would you give, from these two chapters?

12. How does 1:18 – 2:29 enable us to appreciate the gospel?

Pray

Thank God…

- *that he cares enough for his world to judge the people who live in it.*
- *that he knows our hearts, not just how we appear to others.*
- *that in the gospel, there is a way to be right with him.*

Ask God…

- *to give you a truthful self-awareness about your idolatry, and/or religious self-righteousness.*
- *to help you to wrestle with any ways in which this passage has challenged you.*
- *to enable you to change your attitude in any ways that the Spirit is prompting you to.*

3

How to Be Right with God

Romans 3

The Story So Far...

Paul is writing to the Roman church about the gospel: the news that God's righteousness has been revealed by, and can be received from, Jesus.

God's anger is being and will be revealed against all people, unreligious or religious. Religious people judge others for what they themselves do.

Talkabout

1. Have you ever been lost for words? What caused that?

Investigate

📖 **Read Romans 3:1-20**

> **DICTIONARY**
>
> **Nullify** (v 3): make nothing; make invalid.
> **Prevail** (v 4): prove more powerful; win.
> **Fear** (v 18): an attitude of awe at who someone is and/or what they have done.
>
> **Held accountable** (v 19): be called to give a defense for your actions.
> **Conscious** (v 20): aware of.

2. In what sense are Jews and Gentiles—or, we might say, religious and unreligious people—the same (v 9)?

- Some people are clearly less sinful than others. So what does the end of verse 9 mean, do you think?

3. In verses 10-18, Paul gives a long list of sin's effects on us. What are they? (There are at least seven.)

4. How do verses 18-20 sum up the whole of Paul's argument from 1:18?

Getting Personal | OPTIONAL

Verse 19 is speaking of the spiritual condition of silence—knowing that when we stand before God, we will have no defense to make or offer to make. A silent mouth is the spiritual condition of the person who knows that they cannot save themselves. A silent mouth is necessary for us to come to God with empty hands and simply receive his righteousness. In this sense, what keeps people from salvation is not so much their sins but their good works.

Meditate on these truths. Do you know you have nothing to say? Are you truly coming to God with empty hands? Have you received God's righteousness or are you seeking to offer him yours?

Apply

5. Why are verses 18-20 unpopular both inside and outside churches?

- Why are they necessary to understand in order to believe the gospel?

Investigate

📖 **Read Romans 3:21-31**

> **DICTIONARY**
>
> **Testify** (v 21): witness; tell the true facts about.
> **Justified** (v 24): made completely in the right, not guilty.
> **Redemption** (v 24): freedom that costs a price.
> **Sacrifice of atonement** (v 25): literally, propitiation; giving yourself to turn away someone's wrath.
>
> **Forbearance** (v 25): patient self-control.
> **Boasting** (v 27): what you boast in is the thing that gives you confidence, makes you able to face life, and gives you a sense of worth.

6. "A righteousness from God … has been made known" (v 21).
   - How do we get it?

   - Why do we need it?

7. How does Paul describe what Jesus did when he died? What do these verses tell us about *why* he died on the cross?
   - v 24

   - v 25

Explore More | OPTIONAL
📖 **Read Leviticus 16:1-17**
- What was the high priest of Israel, Aaron, to do with a goat (v 5, 15-17)?
- In what way was the animal "presented"?
- What did the sacrifices of the bull (for Aaron) and the goat (for the people) achieve?
- How do the details of Leviticus 16 help us to appreciate further what is meant by "God presented [his Son] as a sacrifice of atonement" (Romans 3:25)?

---

8. On the cross, Jesus, God's Son, died in our place, to take the penalty for our sins. How does this show God to be "just and the one who justifies" sinners who trust in Jesus (v 26)?

9. How does verse 26 help us with these statements?
   - "Of course God will forgive me. He is a loving, forgiving God who forgives as a parent forgives a child."

   - "God could never forgive me after what I've done."

10. Why does being justified by faith mean that "boasting ... is excluded," do you think (v 27)?

11. We've seen (in question 2) that Jews and Gentiles are the same in facing judgment. How else are Jews and Gentiles the same (v 29-30)?

Apply

12. How does believing the gospel ("boasting in Christ")...
    - humble us?

    - enable us to be honest about ourselves?

    - free us from anxiety?

- stop us fearing failure or death?

Getting Personal | OPTIONAL

Which answer to question 12 do you find most liberating?

How will it change the way you look at your life this week?

Pray

Use your answer to question 3 to confess your sins to God.

Use your answer to question 8 to praise God for the gospel.

Use your answer to question 12 to ask God to help you to live out, and enjoy, the justified life.

4

What Abraham and David Discovered

Romans 4

The Story So Far...

Paul is writing to the Roman church about the gospel: the news that God's righteousness has been revealed by, and can be received from, Jesus.

God's anger is being and will be revealed against all people, unreligious or religious. Religious people judge others for what they themselves do.

No one will have any defense to make before God. But we can still be right with him, if we have faith in Jesus, who bore God's just wrath in our place.

Talkabout

1. What is faith? And what good is faith?

Investigate

📖 **Read Romans 4:1-8**

DICTIONARY

Forefather (v 1): ancestor.
Blessedness (v 6): satisfaction and security of living in relationship with God.

Transgressions (v 7): deliberate sins.

An extremely important word in this section is "credited" (also translated "count," v 8). To credit something is to confer a status that was not there before. For instance, some houses can be "leased to buy." You pay rent, but if later you decide to purchase the house, the owner counts your past rent payments as mortgage payments. A new status has been given to those payments—they are credited as mortgage payments.

2. Paul is looking back to the example of Abraham, the ancestor of all Jews. What did Abraham "discover" about being justified (v 1-5)?

- Read Genesis 15:1-6. How does this help us see what "faith" is?

3. Next, Paul looks back to David, the greatest king of Israel. What did David discover about forgiveness (v 6-8)?

Explore More | OPTIONAL

📖 **Read Psalm 32**
- What does this justified-by-faith person do (v 5, 8, 11)?
- Rewrite verses 1-2 and 7 as though David believed he was justified by his works, not his faith.

Apply

4. How would you use verse 5 to explain to someone what saving faith isn't, and is?

5. How is saving faith different from what many churchgoers or religious people think faith is?

Getting Personal | OPTIONAL

Imagine you died tonight, and God said, "Why should I let you into my heaven?" What would you say?

Many would answer, "Because I have tried my best to be a good Christian," or, "Because I believe in God and try to do his will," or, "Because I believe in God with all my heart."

None of these are saving faith. The first is salvation by works; the second salvation by faith and works; the third salvation by faith as a work. True saving faith is a trust transfer: trusting only in God, and not ourselves. It is to answer the question: "Because I believe God's promise to save me."

Do you have saving faith?

Investigate

📖 **Read Romans 4:9-25**

In verses 9-15, Paul is discussing the order of: God crediting Abraham with righteousness; God commanding the family of Abraham to be circumcised; and God giving the family of Abraham his law.

> **DICTIONARY**
>
> **Seal** (v 11): an outward sign of an internal reality.
> **Law** (v 13): here, it is referring to the law God gave Moses on Mount Sinai, around 600 years after Abraham.
> **Offspring** (v 16): children, descendants.
> **Sarah** (v 19): Abraham's wife, who was unable to have children.

6. Why does the order in which these things happened in history matter for how we become righteous?

- What is Paul's conclusion (v 16-17a)?

7. What do we learn about believing God (i.e. having saving faith) in verses 18-22?

- How did Abraham's life show that he knew the truth of the end of verse 17?

8. What does saving faith look like for us today (v 23-25)?

Apply

9. What difference does being justified by faith make?
   - v 2-3

   - v 6-8

   - v 16

   - v 18

10. Share examples, from your own lives or those of Christian friends, of when having faith has resulted in…
    - having hope in a hopeless situation.

- doing something difficult in obedience to God.

11. What is faith, and what good is faith?

Getting Personal | OPTIONAL

If you are trusting in God's promise that Jesus' death and resurrection have justified you…

- which of the answers to question 9 particularly encourages you or comforts you today?
- which aspect of justification by faith are you going to think about, and enjoy, more this week?

Pray

"God … gives life to the dead and calls things that are not as though they were." (4:17)

Use this verse to spend time praising God for all he has done, and is doing, for you.

"Against all hope Abraham … believed … being fully persuaded that God had power to do what he had promised." (v 18, 21)

Pray together for your own faith, that it would be more and more like Abraham's.

Share with each other areas of your lives where you need God to give you this hopeful, promise-trusting faith, and then pray about those things as a group.

5

Enjoying Justification

Romans 5

The Story So Far...

God's anger is being and will be revealed against all people, unreligious or religious. Religious people judge others for what they themselves do.

No one will have any defense to make before God. But we can still be right with him, if we have faith in Jesus, who bore God's just wrath in our place.

Abraham's example shows us that true faith is trusting God's promises; and that God counts those with true faith as right with him.

Talkabout

1. Why is it good to be justified by faith?

Investigate

📖 **Read Romans 5:1-11**

> **DICTIONARY**
>
> **Justified** (v 1): made totally in the right with God, not guilty in any way.
> **Perseverance** (v 3-4): single-minded focus on keeping going.
> **Character** (v 4): here, it means tested-ness.
>
> **Hope** (v 4-5): certainty.
> **Righteous** (v 7): here, Paul likely means self-righteous; someone who thinks they're good.
> **Reconciled** (v 10): brought back into friendship with.

2. What benefits of justification does Paul list in verses 1-2?

3. Imagine someone says, "That's lovely for you—but not for me, because my life is so full of suffering." What does Paul say about the difference being justified makes when we suffer (v 3-5, 11)?

- Why does justification make this difference, do you think?

4. In what two ways can we know that God loves us (v 5-8)?

Apply

5. What difference would it make if verse 3 said...
   - rejoice about our suffering?

   - rejoice beyond suffering?

   - rejoice despite our suffering?

6. How does suffering show where our hopes and dreams are really based?

7. What do we need to remember when we suffer, and remind other Christians about when they suffer?

Getting Personal | OPTIONAL

Think of some specific difficulty or trial you have experienced as a Christian.

Did that time of suffering lead you to focus your attention more on prayer and what you have in God, or less?

Did it cause you to become a more "tested" character—less jittery and fearful?

Did it lead you to a deeper experience of God's presence and love?

If not, was that because you simply did not deliberately spend time with God, or reflect on what he has given you? Was it because you disobeyed him in some way in order to escape the trial? Was it because you felt you were unloved by, or being punished by, God?

Next time you experience hard suffering, what will you do differently or the same as the last time, so that you do rejoice in your suffering as you discover that it is producing perseverance, character, and greater hope in Christ?

Investigate

📖 **Read Romans 5:12-21**

DICTIONARY

One man (v 12): i.e. Adam.
Adam (v 14): the first man, created by God to live in his very good world. (See Genesis 2:4-17.)

Moses (v 14): the man God chose to lead his people out of Egypt, and to whom he gave the law.
Trespass (v 15): Adam trespassed by putting himself in God's place. (See Genesis 3:1-11.)

---

8. How did sin and death enter the world, and who do they affect (v 12-14)?

- How did grace enter the world (v 15)?

Paul is teaching the doctrine of "federal headship"—the truth that we are represented before God by someone else, who acts on our behalf. Western societies are highly individualistic, but the Bible takes a radically different approach—that of human solidarity. This means that you can have a relationship with a person in which whatever they achieve or lose, you do too. They represent you—a little like how if the leader of your country declares war, then you are at war.

In Romans 5, therefore, Paul is saying that all humanity is represented by one of two men: Adam or Christ.

9. How are Adam and Jesus different, in what they did and in the effects their actions had (v 15-17)?

- How are they similar (v 18)?

10. How does verse 19 sum up what Paul has said in verses 12-18?

- Why does "the obedience of the one man," Jesus, matter to us?

Apply

11. Why is it good news that God deals with us through a representative?

12. How would you use Romans 5 to encourage or challenge…
   - a Christian who is unsure they are really loved and saved by God?

   - a Christian who is suffering greatly?

   - a non-believer who is worrying about dying?

   - a non-believer who says, "I'm okay. I'm not a bad person"?

Getting Personal | OPTIONAL

How precious to you is Jesus' obedience as your representative?

How will his obedience on your behalf affect you this week…
   - when you are tempted to sin?
   - when you have sinned?
   - when you are reading a Gospel?
   - when you are praying?

Pray

Thank God for…

Confess to God…

Ask God…

6

Why Christians Obey God

Romans 6:1 - 7:6

The Story So Far...

No one will have any defense to make before God. But we can still be right with him, if we have faith in Jesus, who bore God's just wrath in our place.

Abraham's example shows us that true faith is trusting God's promises; and that God counts those with true faith as right with him.

Being justified means we can enjoy peace with God, access to God, and joy in suffering—all because Christ, our representative, has obeyed on our behalf.

Talkabout

1. Christians are saved by grace, and not by works—so why bother obeying God or living a good life?

Investigate

📖 **Read Romans 6:1-14**

DICTIONARY

Were baptized (v 3): here, Paul means "became Christians."

Count yourselves (v 11): think of yourselves.
Instruments (v 13): tools.

Verse 1 poses the question: *Doesn't the gospel message just encourage us to keep on sinning, so that grace will keep on covering it?*

2. What answer, and what reason, does Paul give in verse 2?

3. How does Paul explain what he means by "[you] died to sin"?
   - v 3-5

   - v 5-7

Paul is taking us to the doctrine of "union with Christ." Everything that has happened to Christ has happened to believers. Everything that is true of Christ is true of believers. Everything that will happen to Christ will happen to believers.

4. Because Christians "died with Christ," what do we now know (v 8-10)?

Explore More | OPTIONAL

📖 **Read Ephesians 1:3-14; 2:1-10**

- What do these passages teach us about what we have "in Christ"—that is, because we are united with him?
- What should our response be (1:3, 6, 12, 14)?

Apply

5. What is the application Paul draws in verses 11-14 for anyone who died with Christ...
   - negatively?

   - positively?

6. "If I fall into sin, it is because I do not realize who I am in Christ." How is this a good summary of Paul's message here?

Getting Personal | OPTIONAL

When a non-Christian sins, they are acting in accord with their identity—why wouldn't they sin? But union with Christ changes everything—changes who we are. When a Christian sins, they are acting against their identity—why would we do that?

What difference does dying with Christ make to your sense of identity? In what area of your life are you finding it hard to "count [yourself] dead to sin but alive to God in Christ Jesus"? How will your identity in Christ help you to live for him?

Investigate

📖 **Read Romans 6:15-23**

DICTIONARY

Impurity (v 19): things which are impure, sinful.

Reap (v 21): harvest.

---

7. Who or what are we free to choose to serve (v 16-18)?

8. How does Paul compare and contrast these two masters?
   - v 19

   - v 21-22

   - v 23

Apply

9. How does this help us to answer these views?
   - "I just couldn't help sinning in that way."

- "I'm determined not to sin. I think to myself, 'Just say no!'"

- "I find myself envying the freedom of my non-Christian friends."

- "God is working in me to change me, so I just let him get on with it."

Investigate

📖 **Read Romans 7:1-6**

Paul now uses another metaphor from everyday 1st-century life. He has explained our relationship to God using the image of slavery; here, he turns to marriage.

DICTIONARY

Bound (v 2): unbreakably joined to.   **Bear** (v 4) and **bore** (v 5): produce(d).

---

10. What does this image teach us about...
    - a believer's relationship to the law?

- a believer's relationship to the Lord Jesus?

11. In what ways does getting married mean being less free? But why is a good marriage still a joy?

- So how are these verses a great motivation to live Jesus' way?

Apply

12. "Since we are saved by grace, why bother obeying God?" How would you answer this question based on the following verses?
    - 6:1-14

    - 6:15-23

- 7:1-6

Getting Personal | OPTIONAL

If you are united to Christ, you are a slave of God and in the most intimate relationship with the Lord Jesus.

How are you currently finding it hard to obey God? How will you use your identity in Christ to motivate you to live for him next time you are tempted to disobey?

Pray

Thank God for the new identity you have in Christ. Spend time in prayer enjoying with him the truth that you are united with his Son.

Ask God to enable you to remember this identity, and live it out in your attitudes and behavior. Speak to him together about areas where you find it hard to obey him, and ask that at those times he would thrill you with your identity in Christ.

7

Warfare Within

Romans 7:7-25

The Story So Far...

Though we deserve judgment, we can be right with God, because Jesus bore God's just wrath in our place. True faith is trusting God's promises in Christ.

Being justified means we can enjoy peace with God, access to God, and joy in suffering—all because Christ, our representative, has obeyed on our behalf.

We don't obey God in order to be saved, but because of who we are: united with Christ, slaves of God, and married to Jesus. Why would we not obey?!

Talkabout

1. Have you ever done something that you had previously decided not to do? What caused you to do it? How did it make you feel?

Investigate

📖 **Read Romans 7:7-13**

Paul has just taught that Christians have been "released from the law" (v 6). So is the law itself a bad thing—is it sinful (v 7)? "Certainly not," says Paul!

DICTIONARY

Coveting (v 7): being discontent about what God has given you, and bitter about what he has given others.

Afforded (v 8): given.

---

2. What does the law do (v 7)?

3. What does sin do as we read the law (v 8-10)?

In verse 9, Paul says, "Once I was alive apart from law." There has been a lot of discussion about what he means! Almost certainly...

Alive = in his self-perception, Paul had felt that he was spiritually alive, pleasing and acceptable to God.

Apart from law = Paul had not realized what the law really required—he saw a lot of rules to keep, but had not understood that the law called for obedience in his attitude. Since he had never seen the law's real demands, he was "apart from law."

4. Why would coveting (i.e. envy) have been the commandment that "killed" Paul, do you think? (Hint: Remember that pre-Christian Paul seems to have focused on keeping the law externally.)

- What happened when Paul really thought about the command "Do not covet" (v 11)?

Explore More | OPTIONAL

📖 **Read Exodus 20:1-17**

- Taking commandments 2 to 9 in turn, what sinful, internal heart-motive lies beneath each wrong behavior God commands us to avoid?

Apply

5. Share examples from your own life when…
   - reading God's law has exposed your sin.

   - your sinfulness has exploited your reading of God's law to encourage you to sin.

Getting Personal | OPTIONAL

Do you allow the law to expose your heart-sins? Do you need to read the law more, reflect on it more, or let it challenge you more?

Investigate

📖 **Read Romans 7:14-25**

Is Paul talking about an unbeliever's or a believer's struggle with sin here? Many thoughtful people have been on both sides of this issue. I think Paul is talking of his own present, Christian experience. He delights in God's law (v 22), he knows he is a lost sinner (v 18), and he knows Christ will rescue him (v 24-25).

> **DICTIONARY**
>
> **Spiritual** and **unspiritual** (v 14): here, Paul means godly and ungodly.
>
> **Members** (v 23): body parts.

6. What is the deepest, "true" Paul like?

- So why is there a struggle?

7. What does Paul conclude about himself (v 24)?

- Do you think this is a fair self-assessment? Why or why not?

8. How can Paul be wretched but not hopeless (v 24-25)?

Apply

9. How does Paul's experience as a Christian both warn and comfort us?

Charles Simeon, the 18th-19th century pastor, wrote, "There are but two objects that I have ever desired … to behold; the one is my own vileness; and the other is the glory of God in the face of Jesus Christ: and I have always thought that they should be viewed together."

10. How is this a good summary of Paul's attitude?

- What prevents us from feeling "wretched" (v 24) about our own vileness?

11. How would you use this passage to…
    - challenge a Christian who is complacent about their sin?

    - encourage a Christian who is burdened by their sin?

Getting Personal | OPTIONAL

There are two forces in the Christian's heart:

- The love of God's law in our deepest self
- The sin in us which hates God's law

Where are these two in most fierce conflict in your life? What does obedience look like in that area?

There are two cries in the Christian's heart:

- Wretchedness about ourselves
- Hope in Christ's rescue

Do you need today to be more honest about your sin, and more wretched in your self-assessment?

Do you need today to be more assured that Christ will rescue you, giving you a perfect body in his sinless world?

Pray

Confess to God your wretchedness. If you're happy to, you might like to share ways in which you are not doing the good you want to do.

Thank God for rescuing you at the cross.

Ask God to enable you to feel your wretchedness when you should, yet never to forget the hope that you have as someone made righteous in Christ.

Romans 1-7

The Gift of God

Leader's Guide: Introduction

This Leader's Guide includes guidance for every question. It will provide background information and help you if you get stuck. For each session, you'll also find the following:

The Big Idea: The main point of the session, in brief. This is what you should be aiming to have fixed in people's minds by the end of the session!

Summary: An overview of the passage you're reading together.

Optional Extra: Usually this is an introductory activity that ties in with the main theme of the Bible study and is designed to break the ice at the beginning of a session. Or it may be a "homework project" that people can tackle during the week.

Occasionally the Leader's Guide includes an extra follow-up question, printed in *italics*. This doesn't appear in the main study guide but could be a useful add-on to help your group get to the answer or go deeper.

Here are a few key principles to bear in mind as you prepare to lead:

- Don't just read out the answers from the Leader's Guide. Ideally, you want the group to discover these answers from the Bible for themselves.

- Keep drawing people back to the passage you're studying. People may come up with answers based on their experiences or on teaching they've heard in the past, but the point of this study is to listen to God's word itself—so keep directing your group to look at the text.

- Make sure everyone finishes the session knowing how the passage is relevant for them. We do Bible study so that our lives can be changed by what we hear from God's word. So, **Apply** questions aren't just an add-on—they're a vital part of the session.

Finally, remember that your group is unique! You should feel free to use this Good Book Guide in a way that works for them. If they're a quiet bunch, you might want to spend longer on the **Talkabout** question. If they love to get creative, try using mind-mapping or doodling to kick-start some of your discussions. If your time is limited, you can choose to skip **Explore More** or split the whole session into two. Adapt the material in whatever way you think will help your group get the most out of God's word.

1

Introducing Righteousness
Romans 1:1-17

The Big Idea
The gospel is about Jesus, about the righteousness of God that he reveals, and which we can receive through him. The gospel makes us eager, not ashamed, to share it.

Summary
This passage contains Paul's introduction of himself (v 1-5); his reasons for wanting to visit the church in Rome that he's writing to (v 8-15); and his outlining of the gospel:
- Who it is about (v 2-4)
- What it does (v 16)
- What it is (v 17)

In fact, the whole passage is about the gospel: Paul is "set apart" for it (v 1), to preach it to the Gentiles (v 5); he wants to visit Rome to encourage the Christians with it (v 11-15); so he is eager about sharing it, rather than ashamed of it (v 15-16).

Verse 17 is crucial for the rest of the letter; it introduces us to the gospel as where God's righteousness is revealed. In other words, the gospel is the way that someone can be brought into right standing before God, where he has nothing against them. The gospel is not merely about forgiveness; it is about being given a perfect record.

NOTE: Verse 17 can be translated "righteousness of God" (i.e. in the gospel, we see God's perfection and holiness) or "righteousness from God" (i.e. in the gospel, we discover a way to be made right with God). Both are true: the gospel is the declaration both that God is righteous, and that he offers that righteousness to anyone who believes.

Optional Extra
Draw up a "mind map" together for the word "gospel." Get a large sheet of paper, write "gospel" in the middle of it, and then ask your group members to say any words or phrases that the word "gospel" prompts in their minds. If you want, you can come back to this mind map throughout the seven studies, referring and adding to it as you go through Romans.

Guidance for Questions

1. **How would you sum up the message of Christianity in one sentence?**
   Encourage members to write down their answer first, before sharing it. You could return to this after question 9. Bear in mind there is more than one correct summary or formulation of the message of Christianity!

2. **How did Paul view himself and his life (v 1, 5)?**
   He is a "servant of Christ Jesus"

(v 1)—he is a man under authority. He has been "called to be an apostle" (v 1)—a "sent one." This is not a job Paul selected himself—he was called into it. He is "set apart for the gospel" (v 1). "Set apart" means separated, moved away, and apart from everything else. To Paul, the gospel is so great that he is willing to separate himself from anything in order to be faithful to his calling. Paul's specific apostolic role is "to call people from among all the Gentiles" (v 5; see Acts 9:15).

3. **What do the first six verses tell us about "the gospel"?**
    - v 2: *Its origin*. It is not a new thing; the Old Testament ("Holy Scriptures") was all about it.
    - v 3-4: *Its subject*. The gospel centers on Jesus—it is all "regarding his Son." It is about him, not us. Jesus is: human (v 3); the fulfillment of God's promises to David of an eternal king (v 3; see 2 Samuel 7:11b-16); and divine (Romans 1:4—the resurrection is the proof of this claim).
    - v 5-6: *Its result*. The gospel causes an obedience to God (v 5; see question 4); and enables us to "belong" to Jesus.

4. **What does true faith result in (v 5)?**
    Obedience. The gospel calls us both to obey Christ and to trust Christ (obedience and faith).
    - **Why is this, do you think?**
    The rest of Romans will explain what this means! But it does not mean that Paul is teaching that to be saved, someone must have both faith and obedience. This obedience "comes from" faith; it flows out of it and is a consequence of having saving faith, but it is not a second condition for salvation. Second, it means that true faith will bring obedience. The gospel is the declaration that Jesus is the promised King and risen Son of God, and that there is salvation under his rule. Therefore, true faith is faith in a divine King, to whom we (like Paul) are servants (v 1). Faith will always bring joyful obedience to our loving King.

5. **Who is Paul writing to (v 7)? How does he describe them?**
    Roman Christians; people who are loved by God; called to be saints (i.e. distinctive, holy, set apart); and who therefore enjoy grace from, and peace with, God.

- **How is he praying for them (v 8-10)?**
    - He thanks God for their faith (v 8).
    - He prays for them regularly ("at all times," v 10).
    - He's praying that he will be able to visit them (v 10).
- ○ *OPTIONAL: What can we learn from this for our own prayers?*
- **Why does he want to visit them (v 11-13)?**
    To use his spiritual gifts (i.e. his abilities of preaching and pastoring) to encourage them in their faith. He also expects to be encouraged by

their faith too. He wants to have "a harvest among you"—likely he is referring to the harvest of growth in maturity within the church, and to evangelism and conversions outside the church.

6. **How can we mutually encourage each other as Christians today?**

   By spending time together—by committing to being in church gatherings on Sundays, and seeking to see one another at other times, too. But to know this encouragement as we meet, we need to remember that time spent with other believers is time spent with those who know (like us) that Jesus is God's Son, raised with power to rule in power. We will be encouraged by seeing others' faith, and the obedience that flows from it. We will see others using their gifts for others, and we are able to use ours for them. So we can mutually encourage each other by meeting together, and intentionally expecting both to encourage and be encouraged.

7. **How does Paul feel about the gospel (v 15)? How does he not feel (v 16)?**

   He is eager; he is not ashamed (or, literally, "offended").

- **Why might people have a view of the gospel that is opposite from Paul's view?**
  - The gospel tells us that we are such spiritual failures that the only way to gain salvation is for it to be a complete gift. This offends moral and religious people who think their decency gives them an advantage over less moral people.
  - The gospel is also really insulting by telling us that Jesus died for us; that we are so wicked that only the death of the Son of God could save us. This offends the modern cult of self-expression and the popular belief in the innate goodness of humanity.
  - The gospel, by telling us that "trying to be good and spiritual isn't enough," insists that no "good" person will be saved. This offends the modern notion that any nice person anywhere can find God "in his own way." We don't like losing our autonomy.
  - The gospel tells us that our salvation was accomplished by Jesus' suffering and serving (not conquering and destroying), and that following him means to suffer and serve with him. This offends people who want salvation to be an easy life.

8. **Why is Paul *not* ashamed (v 14, 16)?**

   It is better to take verse 16 first.
   - The gospel is God's power. When it is proclaimed, God is powerfully at work. It lifts people up; it transforms and changes things. If we take it in personally, it is not merely an idea or philosophy. It changes us and changes others. Paul knows that as he shares the gospel, there is nothing to be embarrassed about, and everything to be excited about!

- The gospel is the power of God "for ... salvation." It can do what nothing else can do: save us, reconcile us to God, and guarantee us a place in the kingdom of God forever. It is the message that everyone (Jew and Gentile) needs and can trust in.
- v 14 —Paul is "obligated" ("bound," NIV84UK), or indebted, by the gospel message. He is in debt to those who have not yet heard it, because God gives us the gospel to pass on the gospel.

9. **Put Paul's nutshell summary of the Christian message from verse 17a into your own words.**

   Of course, each summary will vary. A key word here is "righteousness," which simply means to be in right standing with someone—you owe nothing to them. You are acceptable to someone else, because your record has nothing on it to damage or destroy your relationship with them.

   Point out also that "righteousness from God" (NIV84) can also be translated "righteousness of God" (NIV2011)—see Summary on p. 55. The gospel tells us that God gives us his perfect record. Salvation is not about us providing our righteousness to God but about us receiving God's righteousness from God.

   So, one summary would be: "In the gospel, God shows us and provides for us a perfectly righteous record, which is received by faith, and by faith alone."

Explore More

○ **Who is the gospel for (v 14, 16)? Why does Paul underline this truth, do you think?**
   Greeks and non-Greeks; wise and foolish (v 14); Jew and Gentile (v 16). That is, everyone—no matter how "high" or "low," or "religious" or "unreligious." He is underlining it is not just for an "elite."

○ **Who does the gospel save (v 16-17)?**
   Everyone who believes; righteousness is received "by faith."

○ **What happens if we forget...**

○ **the unlimited nature of the gospel message?**
   We will think that some people are too bad for God to be willing to save them, or that others are too stubborn for God to be able to save them. We will stop sharing the gospel with particular types or groups of people.

○ **that people are not saved if they do not believe that message?**
   We will grow complacent and stop sharing the gospel, since we will think that certain types of people (or all people) are acceptable to God even if they do not believe the gospel.

○ **Which are you more likely to forget?**

10. **What does the end of verse 17 remind us about the Christian life?**
    It is "by faith." We do not begin the Christian life through faith, and

then continue it by our own performance. Since perfect righteousness can only ever be received, we go on in the Christian life as we started it; receiving God's righteousness and salvation by faith.

11. **What have verses 14-17 taught us about...**
    - **the debt of the gospel?**
      We are obliged to share the gospel. A helpful illustration is to think about how someone can be in debt by $100. There are two ways. I could give you $100, and you would be in debt to me. Or I could give you $100 and ask you to give it to someone else; now, you are in debt to them, until you give them the $100. God gives us the gospel to pass on to others—we are in debt to them until we do. The gospel message obliges us to share it.

    - **the power of the gospel?**
      It is God's power! It changes people; it works as it is heard or read.

    - **the content of the gospel?**
      It is about Jesus—about how, in him, God's perfection (righteousness) is both seen by us, and offered to us, to be received by faith.

    - **Why would forgetting any of these lead us to keep quiet about the gospel?**
      - We would leave gospel sharing to others.
      - We would doubt that our gospel sharing would ever make any difference.
      - We would forget how wonderful, and necessary, the gospel is.

12. **In what ways can we forget that "the righteous will live by faith" in the gospel?**
    At the root of each and every sin, and each and every problem, is unbelief and a rejection of the gospel. People who are immoral and people who are moral both reject the gospel when they try to be their own savior.
    - When licentious people reject religion and God, their rebellion is really a refusal to believe the gospel—the message that they are so sinful, that only Jesus can be their Savior.
    - When moralistic people pick up religion and morality and become either anxious (because they are aware they can never live up to the standards) or proud (because they think they have), their anxiety and/or pride is really a refusal to believe the gospel—the message that they are so sinful that only Jesus can be their Savior.
    - When Christian people sin, it always involves forgetting that they cannot save themselves; only Jesus can. When we are bitter, it is because we have forgotten that we are already totally saved by grace alone—so how can we withhold grace? When we are overworking out of fear of failure, or depressed because we have failed, it is because we have forgotten that we cannot earn our own righteousness, but in God's eyes we are righteous.

2

Why Everyone Needs the Gospel

Romans 1:18 - 2:29

The Big Idea
God's anger is being and will be revealed against all people, whether unreligious or religious—we all need the gospel.

Summary
The NIV translations leave out the word "For" which should come at the beginning of verse 18. The word connects this section with verses 16-17; in other words, in this section Paul is going to explain *why* we need to receive God's righteousness by faith.

The answer is that God's wrath is being poured out. It is working now, against the godlessness of people who are suppressing the truth about God. It is seen in the way we are "given over" to the things we worship instead of God. Idolatry is both the cause of, and the consequence of, God's wrath. We choose to worship created things (v 21-23); they do not satisfy, and instead lead to brokenness; and God's present wrath is to let us have what we have chosen.

In 1:18-32, Paul is addressing the Gentile (i.e. non-Jewish, or we might say, non-religious world). In 2:1, he turns to the religious or moral person. These people would support Paul's critique of the pagan world and lifestyle. But they would have assumed that they themselves (since they weren't unreligious) were not under condemnation. In 2:1-10 (and right up to 3:20), Paul shows the Jews and all religious people that they are condemning themselves by the standards they insist others should keep (2:1-3); they deserve wrath too (v 3-5); they have missed the whole point of the gospel, because they think their own goodness makes them righteous, and so they have no need to receive it. Everyone—both unreligious and religious—needs the gospel.

Optional Extra
Write out on slips of paper the names of between 15 and 20 famous people, ranging from the very good (e.g. Roosevelt, Churchill), and the very religious (e.g. Billy Graham, Mother Teresa), to the very bad (Hitler, bin Laden), via the "normal" (a sports or film star, an author, perhaps you!) Ask the group to order them in terms of their goodness, or acceptability in your society. Then, as you go through the study, refer back to your order. Romans 1:18-32 suggests that God may draw a line between religious and/or good people who acknowledge his existence, and everyone else. 2:1-10 reveals that in fact God draws a line above everyone—no one is right with him.

Guidance for Questions

1. **If you asked 100 people, "What is wrong with the world?" what answers would you get?**
   Some possibilities: greed, selfishness, climate change, nothing much, our failure to love one another properly.

   - **If you asked those people, "What would fix what is wrong?" what answers would you get?**
   This is a harder question to answer. Don't let the discussion go on too long. But most answers will tend toward arguing that there is no solution or that the solution lies within ourselves—humanity can fix humanity's problems.

2. **What do verses 18-21 tell us about God's wrath?**
   - *It exists.* A loving God is also a wrathful God. Wrath is justified, fair anger. It is an outworking of God's love for his world that he is angry about what is wrong in it.
   - *It is present.* It is here, working now (note the present tense "is being revealed," v 18). The rest of chapter 1 shows how it is being revealed.
   - *What it is against.* It is versus "godlessness" (v 18) (a word that refers to a disregard of God's rights) and "wickedness" (meaning a disregard of human rights to love, justice, truth, etc.).
   - *It is deserved.* God is wrathful toward those who know better, who "suppress the truth." Every person, deep down, knows there is a God to whom they owe allegiance and obedience. God has "made it plain to them … since the creation of the world" (v 19-20). Creation shows us there is a God, but although we know this, we don't live for him or thank him (v 21). We are all "without excuse" (v 20) for living as though there is no God.

3. **Paul is talking about humans who reject the knowledge and worship of God. What does he say always happens to people who do this (v 22-25)?**
   - *Counterfeit-god construction.* Paul uses two words in verse 25: we "worship" and "serve" created things. We were created to worship the Creator so, if we reject him, we will worship something. Whatever we worship we will "serve" or have to obey. Something must have the highest priority to give us meaning. Whatever that is, we "serve" it.
   - *Bondage and addiction.* Paul says, "Therefore God gave them over in the sinful desires of their hearts" (v 24). The things we serve will not free us. Rather, they control us. We are "given over to them." We have to have them in order to be happy, to like ourselves, to have meaning in life. And since they do not satisfy (because our hearts were made to center on God, not on any created thing), we always need more and more.

4. What are some of the consequences of not wanting to know God (v 26-32)?

Here, Paul is showing us that false worship leads to the complete disintegration of human life. Encourage your group to think about what each consequence looks like in life, rather than simply reading out the list.

- *Bondages and addictions* (v 26, 28, "gave them over to shameful lusts") because a false god becomes a tyrant that can never be satisfied.
- *Disordered relationships* (v 26-27—see note below). "Due penalty" (v 27) likely means that God responds to a decision not to live according to his commandments by allowing that decision to be made. This is God's wrath—the penalty of not living with him as God is to experience the consequences of that way of life.
- *Decay of personal and corporate life* (v 29-31) because behavior deteriorates:
  a. Economic disorder ("greed")
  b. Social disorder ("murder, strife, deceit and malice")
  c. Family breakdown ("they disobey their parents")
  d. Relational breakdown ("gossips, slanderers … insolent, arrogant and boastful")
  e. Character breakdown ("senseless, faithless, heartless, ruthless")

There are also two consequences in verse 21:

- *Intellectual confusion and frustration* (futile reasoning) because to deny the supremacy of the true God requires holding to many contradictory beliefs.
- *Emotional confusion and frustration* (darkened hearts) because the heart and desires were originally built for God and nothing else put on the throne of the heart will satisfy.

NOTE: Verses 26-27 see homosexuality as a sexual bondage that flows out of idolatry. You should know three things:

- This is the longest passage in the Bible on homosexuality.
- This calls homosexuality "against nature" (*para phusin*). This means it is a violation of the nature God gave us.
- This says homosexuality comes from worshiping the creature rather than the Creator. We have seen that every problem comes from idolatry of some kind, so homosexuality isn't the only one. Active homosexuality is a sin; but it is not the only sin, nor is it more serious than other sin. All sin is a suppression of the truth about God, and a worshiping of something else in his place; and this is what brings his wrath.

5. How do we see the reality of God's present wrath in the world around us?

God's revealed wrath is the cause of the disintegration we see all around. Because God's punishment is simply to "give us over" (v 24a, 26a, 28a) to the things we worship and want, the reality of God's wrath is seen in the fact that we do just that—worship created things and look for our meaning and purpose in them. So God's wrath is seen in the person who, having rejected the truth, cannot understand who Jesus is; the person who has made choices in their life which have left them disappointed or despairing; the father who doesn't see his family because he is chasing the promotion he "must have"; and so on. When we sin, it sets up strains in the fabric of life in God's world, and leads to breakdowns spiritually, psychologically, socially, and physically.

6. **Do you think your church community is less prone to this truth-suppression and idol-worship than the surrounding culture? Why do you think this?**
It is very easy for professing Christians to exempt themselves, at least to some extent, from Paul's appraisal of humanity here. Of course, it is equally possible for us to locate our own sins in this list. So members of your group may answer this question in one of two ways: "Yes, we know the truth about God and so we don't worship idols as much"; or "Yes, we are just as sinful as those around us." As we will see, Paul challenges the first view in Romans 2.

7. **What kind of person is Paul addressing in verses 1-3? (Verse 17 may help.)**
People who "pass judgment on someone else" (v 1); who "call [themselves] a Jew ... rely on the law" (v 17). These are religious people who rely on their own observance of God's standards to make themselves acceptable to him. These are people who would read chapter 1 and say: "Yes, of course God's wrath lies on the ungodly people who don't come to church. But we have the word of God and we live by it. We are not condemned."

- **What point is he making to them?**
"You are condemning yourself, because you ... do the same things" (v 1). Paul is saying that the standards we use on others will be the standards by which we are judged. To pass judgment is to believe that others are worthy of judgment but you are not; but Paul says that none of us keep to the standards we hold others to.

It is what the 20th-century theologian Francis Schaeffer called the "invisible tape recorder." It is as though there is a tape recorder (nowadays it would be a mobile phone!) around each of our necks. It records the things we say to others and about others, about how they ought to live. Then, at the last day, God the Judge will take the tape recorder off your neck and say, *I will be completely fair—I will simply play this tape and judge you on the basis of what your own words say are the standards for human behavior.* Paul asks, "Do you think you will escape God's judgment" (v 3)? No one in history can truthfully answer, "Yes, I do."

- **What does he warn them of (v 4-5)?**
  God is kindly giving self-righteous people more time so that they might come to "repentance" (v 4)—i.e. realize that they are sinners, and so turn to trust in the gospel. But for as long as they don't repent, "you are storing up wrath against yourself for the day of God's wrath" in the future (v 5). The longer we get God's blessings without repenting, the greater the final punishment.

Explore More

- **What is the first group like (Psalm 62:3-4)? What have they "done" in terms of how they relate to God?**
  They plot against God's chosen king (i.e. David, the writer); they lie, saying one thing with their lips while doing the opposite in their hearts. They are like the people in Romans 2:1-3.

- **What have the second group "done" (v 1, 7)?**
  Looked to God for their salvation (v 1); placed all they have in God, relying on him for their rescue and reputation (v 7).

- **So what does David mean in verse 12, when he says each group will be rewarded "according to what [they have] done"?**
  That God will "reward" the first type of person by judging them for their attitude of rejecting God; and "reward" the second type by giving them the blessings and salvation they are relying on him for.

- **How does this help us understand Paul in Romans 2:6-11?**
  Paul is asking the religious and unreligious man to consider what they have "done"—or, rather, not done. Neither has repented (v 5), seeking refuge from God's wrath in God's undeserved mercy. Both are seeking honor in themselves.

- **What is the challenge here for professing Christians?**
  Do our lives reflect the faith we profess? If the works of our hands are not being changed and informed by the faith we claim to have, we should ask ourselves honestly whether our faith is real.

8. **How does he show that there is no defense before God for...**

- **unreligious people (v 13-16)?**
  Verses 14-15 are key here. When people who haven't heard the law (Gentiles) "do ... things required by the law ... they show that the requirements of the law are written on their hearts."

  God's law is inborn in people—all people know the essential principles of right and wrong and their basis in an objective reality, a standard by which we are to be judged. The fact that people who have never heard God's law sometimes know that something is right, and therefore do it, shows that they have no excuse for the times when they do not do what is right—their own thoughts sometimes accuse and sometimes defend them (v 15).

NOTE: This is a complicated section; don't get sidetracked by trying to understand all its complexities.

- **religious people (v 17-27)?**
  Verses 17-24 are about moral behavior; verses 25-27 are about religious observance. Again, the point here is that religious people do not practice what they preach (v 21). One example Paul gives is adultery (v 21). Religious people are severe on others who commit adultery. But Jesus said adultery includes our thoughts (Matthew 5:28). Godly living is about the heart motives as much as (or more than) the actions of the body. Knowing and teaching the law does not stop someone disobeying the law themselves, and therefore being worthy of judgment.

  In verses 25-27, Paul mentions circumcision. This was the great cultural marker of Jewishness, which identified members of God's people. But it had become part of Jewish pride, part of a complacent assumption that being circumcised made you automatically right with God. But Paul says that the only thing that matters is keeping the law or breaking the law. If someone is a law-breaker (as everyone is—v 1-3), then circumcision has no value (v 25) in saving them.

9. **What is the only thing that really matters (v 28-29)?**
   Whether or not your heart is "circumcised," i.e. brought into God's true people, through the work of the Spirit in enabling us to trust the gospel message.

- **What does this kind of heart result in, both negatively and positively (end of verse 29)? Why, do you think?**
  Not praise from men, but praise from God. When God looks at someone in whom his Spirit has worked to enable them to receive his Son's righteousness, he sees them as one of his, as someone completely acceptable, as an object of praise, not condemnation. A Christian may not receive praise from men (either for rejection of God, or for outwardly religious purity), but when we know we have God's approval and praise, man's opinion ceases to have a hold on us.

10. **How would we know if we were the "you" Paul is addressing in chapter 2?**
    Paul points us to four things:
    - A theoretical-only stance toward the word of God (v 21: "You ... who teach others, do you not teach yourself?"). This person understands the concepts of the gospel, but these never change them. They are rarely struck by a deep conviction of their sin. A real Christian finds the Bible "living and active" (Hebrews 4:12); they find it convicts, comforts, thrills, challenges, and changes them. They read their Bible to teach themselves.

- Subtle or obvious moral superiority (v 17: "You … brag;" v 19: "A light for those who are in the dark"). If you are relying on your spiritual achievements (morality and/or religious observance), you will have to "look down" on those who have failed in the same areas. People relying on their own goodness are at least "cold" and at worst very judgmental toward those who are struggling. And they tend to gossip (putting others down allows them to see themselves as better) and be very defensive (because they can't admit to flaws or mistakes).
- Most importantly, a total lack of an "inner life" (v 29: "circumcision of the heart, by the Spirit"). A circumcised heart is one spiritually melted and softened. It means to have an active prayer life, a sense of the presence and nearness of God. That is something that moralists do not have regularly. They may get "feelings" when they are caught up in the liturgy or the excitement of a church service, but they are radically unsure that God loves them, so they experience a long-term deadness within. (NOTE: This is not to say that a real Christian always has great quiet times, or always feels like praying!)
- There may be outright hypocrisy and a double life (v 22). It is possible that a "pillar of the church" is having an affair or is dishonest in business.

11. **If someone asked you, "What is wrong with the world?" what answer would you give, from these two chapters?**

    The very short answer is: sin. The longer answer from these chapters is that we all suppress the truth about God and worship something else, either religiously, where we worship our own goodness, or unreligiously. This means we hurt ourselves and hurt others in our pursuit of what we have decided we must have (be it a particular sexual experience, being able to feel self-righteous and "good enough," or something else).

12. **How does 1:18 – 2:29 enable us to appreciate the gospel?**

    The gospel is necessary not simply to make us happy but because there is such a thing as the wrath of God. All of Paul's confidence, joy, and passion for the gospel (1:1-17) rests on the assumption that all human beings are, apart from the gospel, under God's wrath. If you don't understand or believe in the wrath of God, and that you deserve to face it, the gospel will not thrill, empower, or move you.

3

How to Be Right with God

Romans 3

The Big Idea
Based on our own performance, we have no defense or excuse before God; but God offers to make us right with him by judging Jesus in our place, demonstrating both his justice and his mercy.

Summary
In the first 20 verses of chapter 3, Paul is concluding his argument that everyone needs the gospel, because "no one [is] righteous" (3:10). So no one will be able to say anything in their defense when they are held accountable by God (3:19).

So the first two words of verse 21 are wonderful: "But now..." At the cross, God has made his righteousness—his perfection—available to anyone who trusts in Jesus' death. The cross is where God justly punishes sin in his Son, and therefore where he can make righteous ("justify") sinners.

NOTE: There are a number of technical words in this section, particularly in verses 21-31. Short definitions are given in the Dictionary boxes in the Study Guide, and longer ones in the answers below.

Optional Extra
Ask everyone to draw up a "resumé," containing their top three in these categories: proudest achievements; most precious relationships; best qualities; biggest regrets/mistakes (no one else will see). Then, after question 10 or 11, point out that nothing on that list makes them righteous; and nothing stops them receiving righteousness. All that matters for righteousness is to have on our resumé: *I have faith in Christ's blood.*

Guidance for Questions

1. Have you ever been lost for words? What caused that?

Question 4 and the subsequent Getting Personal speak of the spiritual condition of silence—this is a fun way of introducing it. You could return to question 1 after question 4, or after the Getting Personal section.

2. In what sense are Jews and Gentiles—or, we might say, religious and unreligious people—the same (v 9)?

We are all "under sin" i.e. unrighteous. (See verse 10.) No one is blameless with respect to God and others; we have wronged both God and others, and so are in their debt. Both "good" and "bad" people are "alike" under sin.

- **Some people are clearly less sinful than others. So what does the end of verse 9 mean, do you think?**

We are not all as sinful as everybody else. But we are all sinful, and

67

therefore all lost. A helpful illustration: three people try to swim from Hawaii to Japan (3,850 miles). One manages 10 yards before drowning. Another swims a mile, then drowns. The third is a very strong swimmer, and gets 10 miles before drowning. They are not equally weak swimmers; but all are equally drowned. In the same way, everyone, though not equally sinful, is equally "under sin," facing the same condemnation.

3. **In verses 10-18, Paul gives a long list of sin's effects on us. What are they? (There are at least seven.)**
   - *Our legal standing* (v 10). No one is right with God; all are guilty. (See question 2.)
   - *Our minds* (v 11). There is no one who understands, because sin has darkened our thinking about spiritual issues. (See 1:21-23; Ephesians 4:18.)
   - *Our motives* (v 11). None of us truly want to find God—though we may seek what we think he will give us, left to ourselves we do not seek him for himself. (NOTE: This means that none of us sought God before he sought us, through his Spirit.)
   - *Our will* (v 12). "Turned away" is probably referring to Isaiah 53:6— "All we like sheep have gone astray; we have turned every one to his own way" (KJV). We are willful; we demand self-determination, the right to choose our own paths.
   - *Our tongues* (v 13-14). Our words are signs of the decay within (and cause it). Our tongues deceive and harm ("cursing").
   - *Our relationships* (v 15-17). Instead of being at peace with others, we are "after their blood"—we are self-centered, seeking what we can from others, and fighting those who get in our way.
   - *Our attitude to God* (v 18). The "fear of God" is not cringing fear; it is an inner attitude of awe, respect, and trembling joy at how great God is. Sin is the opposite of this: to willfully control our own lives, to look to and exalt our own greatness, and seek to save ourselves.

4. **How do verses 18-20 sum up the whole of Paul's argument from 1:18?**
   - v 18: As we saw in question 3, no one has a right attitude to God, respecting him for who he is and what he has done in saving us.
   - v 19a: Everyone is accountable. The law applies to everyone who seeks to keep it as much as everyone who doesn't.
   - v 19b-20: No one has any defense to make. The law is not given so we can declare ourselves righteous; it is the way we realize we are sinful. The law is not a checklist we keep; it is a benchmark we fail. The right response to knowing the law is to realize that we are in desperate trouble, and that our "mouth [will] be silenced"(v 19). Whoever we are, we have no defense or offer to make to God—we face condemnation.

5. **Why are verses 18-20 unpopular both inside and outside churches?**

   Because no one likes to be told that all people will be held to account by God, and that they cannot survive that reckoning left to themselves. These verses are offensive to…
   - liberal people, who reject the idea of absolute right and wrong, and of judgment.
   - churchgoing people, who reject the idea that good deeds cannot wholly merit, or even contribute to, acceptance before God.
   - people of other religions.
   - our own hearts: we may accept this truth in our heads, but not apply it to our loved ones who are very good to us, but who are not trusting in Christ.

- **Why are they necessary to understand in order to believe the gospel?**

   If we don't know we need a rescue, then we will never accept the rescue that is offered. The gospel will be closed to us; it will not move or thrill us. The gospel only makes sense if: (a) there is a judgment coming and (b) no one will be declared righteous through their own works.

6. **"A righteousness from God … has been made known" (v 21).**
- **How do we get it?**

   "Through faith in Jesus Christ" (v 22); "through faith in his blood" (v 25). So we receive right standing with God…
   - by faith, not by our own efforts ("apart from law," v 21; "for all have sinned and fall short," v 23).
   - by faith in Christ, not faith in general. Someone is not saved by having faith in general, or even faith in the God of the Bible but by faith in Jesus Christ.
   - by faith in Christ's work on the cross, not general admiration of him. Some people say, "I believe in Jesus," when they mean a belief in him as an example or as a help. That is not saving faith.
   - by faith as a way of receiving, not as a work. We are "justified freely." Faith is not something we do that earns righteousness. It is trust in what someone else—Jesus—has done.

   o *OPTIONAL: These questions will help you draw out the specific aspects of how we receive righteousness:*
   o *What details does Paul add to the word "faith"?*
   o *What definitions of "faith" do those extra details rule out?*

- **Why do we need it?**

   Verse 23: all have sinned and fallen short of God's glory.

7. **How does Paul describe what Jesus did when he died? What do these verses tell us about *why* he died on the cross?**
- **v 24**

   He redeemed us—freed us by paying a price. You may want to explain that redemption is a word that takes us back to Old Testament Israel. In that agricultural society, it did not take much to get into debt, into having to sell yourself into slavery, but it did take much—your whole life, perhaps—to get out of it. So God's law made provision for a kinsman-redeemer—a *go'el*—who would buy you out of that debt, that slavery, so you could live free again (Leviticus 25:25). Now Paul says that through Jesus, we can be freed from the debt we owe, and no longer be slaves to death and judgment.

- **v 25**
  He was "a sacrifice of atonement" (v 25). The Greek word is *hilastrion*—"propitiation," to turn away wrath. God's anger is turned away from us—those who deserve it—by the provision of one who takes it in our place—God himself, Jesus. God punished sinful humans in the person of his Son, the sinless man Jesus. Our punishment has been paid by Christ, so we can receive right standing with God.

Explore More

- **What was the high priest of Israel, Aaron, to do with a goat (Leviticus 16:5, 15-17)?**
- **In what way was the animal "presented"?**
  Take two goats (v 5; one was for another purpose—see verses 20-22); then kill one and sprinkle its blood on "the atonement cover" (this was on the top of the ark of the covenant, where God dwelled among his people in the center of the tabernacle), and sprinkle more blood on the Tent of Meeting (where God met with people to speak with them, Exodus 29:42-43).

- **What did the sacrifices of the bull (for Aaron) and the goat (for the people) achieve?**
  Atonement—i.e. the restoring of relationship between God and the sinful (v 16) people. The goat died so that the people, who deserved to die, didn't have to—and (as the book of Hebrews explains in detail), this death pointed to the atonement that Christ's death would achieve.

- **How do the details of Leviticus 16 help us to appreciate further what is meant by "God presented [his Son] as a sacrifice of atonement" (Romans 3:25)?**
  Jesus was a sacrifice presented by God, not by man—it was his plan and his action. Ultimately, Jesus was the only atoning sacrifice. As the goat died in place of the Israelite community, so that they could be in relationship with (rather than punished by) God, so Jesus died in place of all of his people—he pacified the wrath of God the Father.

8. **On the cross, Jesus, God's Son, died in our place, to take the penalty for our sins. How does this show God to be "just and the one**

who justifies" sinners who trust in Jesus (v 26)?

God is just—he promises to uphold his standards and punish sin and, at the cross, he did punish sin. The cross demonstrates God's justice, that he does punish sinful humanity.

Yet at the cross, God also justifies sinners, because he punishes their sin in Jesus. Since their sin has already been judged and punished, they are now legally not guilty, with no punishment to bear.

At the cross, both God's wrath and love are fully demonstrated and satisfied.

9. **How does verse 26 help us with these statements?**

- **"Of course God will forgive me. He is a loving, forgiving God who forgives as a parent forgives a child."**

  This is to depict our relationship with God far too simplistically. God is not only a Father to his people; he is also King and Judge of the universe. And deep down, we want him to be a God who judges sin. A God who simply forgave without judging would be a God who was indifferent to suffering, and whose word could not be trusted. Of course we want to be forgiven by God; but we all want God to judge too. He will not stop being just in order to be forgiving, and his forgiveness does not come automatically. It comes by Jesus dying in our place. We receive it through believing that Jesus died for us, personally.

- **"God could never forgive me after what I've done."**

  You are right to think that what you've done should leave you facing judgment, and right that there must be a consequence. And God cannot and will not simply forgive you. But he has made a way for the consequences to be laid on himself, in the person of his Son. On the cross, God bore his own judgment so that you and I don't have to face it. Don't underestimate God's achievement at the cross! There is no one who does not need to be forgiven by trusting that Jesus has borne their sins; there is no one whose sin God cannot or will not forgive if they ask Jesus to take the penalty for it.

10. **Why does being justified by faith mean that "boasting … is excluded," do you think (v 27)?**

    Make sure people understand what "boasting" is. It is the thing that gives you your confidence as you face the day; the characteristic, ability, relationship, etc. that is the root of your identity. But if we are justified by faith, we realize that nothing we are or have or can do is any use in making us right with God. Even our best achievements have done nothing to justify us. There is nothing in us to boast about. The only thing that has given us righteousness is something someone else has done—Jesus, on the cross. Paul is saying that boasting in yourself and believing in the gospel are opposites; you can't do both.

11. **We've seen (in question 2) that Jews and Gentiles are the same in facing judgment. How else are Jews and Gentiles the same (v 29-30)?**

   In salvation. God is the God of the whole world, Jews and Gentiles, and he justifies anyone, circumcised or not, "through [the] same faith" (v 30).

   o *OPTIONAL: Substitute "religious and unreligious" or "good and bad" for "Jews and Gentiles." What is Paul underlining in verses 29-30?*

   That it is faith, and only faith, that means someone can receive righteousness, whoever you are and whatever your background.

12. **How does believing the gospel ("boasting in Christ")...**

   - **humble us?**

   The best we do or are is nothing to be proud about or to rely on, because it cannot justify us. The sum of our best efforts and greatest achievements would still leave us sinful, facing judgment.

   - **enable us to be honest about ourselves?**

   We do not need to cover up our sin from ourselves, others, and God; it has been fully dealt with at the cross. We don't need to pretend that we are good people, since we know we are not, and that we don't need to be. In fact, if we understand what Christ has done for us, we will want others to know we are sinful, and we will want to acknowledge that ourselves, so that we can point away from ourselves to Jesus and say, *I am a sinner, but Jesus still saved me!*

   - **free us from anxiety?**

   You don't need to be afraid of the future, because God is for you. You can place your worst fears into his hands and leave them there, knowing that if he justified you while you were a rebel, he will be for you as his child. You face difficulties by saying, *I know God wouldn't go to all the trouble of justifying me at the cross and then not give me what I really need now.*

   - **stop us fearing failure or death?**

   Our worst failure does not affect our standing before God at all—that relies completely on Christ's obedient life and sin-bearing death. If a failing causes others to turn away from us, we will still be loved by the only one in the universe whose opinion of us matters eternally. And we do not need to fear death, since we know that beyond it lies a welcome from the God we are now right with. We do not need to fear judgment, because we have Christ's righteousness as our righteousness.

4

What Abraham and David Discovered

Romans 4

The Big Idea
Abraham's example shows us that true faith is trusting God's promises; and that God counts those with true faith as right with him.

Summary
Having laid out the gospel—that through the cross, God is just and the justifier of those who have faith in Christ's blood—Paul now turns to two Old Testament "witnesses," Abraham and David.

This is a masterstroke from Paul. Abraham is the father of the Jewish nation, and the Jews at the time held him up as a man of great obedience—and therefore righteous. But Paul says that in fact, Abraham "discovered" that it was his faith in God's promises that were reckoned to him as right standing with God—and Scripture proves it, in Genesis 15:6, which Paul quotes (Romans 4:3). Abraham is a great example of saving faith.

Further, so is David, Israel's greatest king. Paul quotes from one of David's psalms in order to show that blessing comes from confessing sin and being forgiven. Paul then returns to the life of Abraham, pointing out the following:

- Abraham was righteous before he was circumcised—so circumcision cannot be a condition of being justified (v 9-12).
- The law was given after Abraham's life—so obedience to the law of Moses cannot be a condition, either (v 13-17).
- Abraham's life shows us that the faith that is credited as righteous is a faith that believes God's promises despite appearances or weakness (v 18-22).
- Saving faith today means believing God's promise that Christ's death and resurrection justify us (v 23-25).

Optional Extra
Ask group members to think about their family trees. Talk about any interesting ancestors, especially any you are particularly proud to count in your family, and any more recent family members who you feel you share characteristics with, or who you would like to be similar to. Link into the study by explaining how important family and people were to the Jewish nation—particularly such great ancestors as Abraham and David. There was huge respect and fierce pride for such men; what they did, and said, and believed mattered greatly.

Guidance for Questions

1. **What is faith? And what good is faith?**

   The first of these questions is asking

for a definition, the second for the consequences of having faith. This study ends (question 11) with the same questions—a chance for your group to consider what they have learned or been reminded of.

2. **Paul is looking back to the example of Abraham, the ancestor of all Jews. What did Abraham "discover" about being justified (v 1-5)?**
   - v 3: Being justified (becoming righteous—the two words are translated from the same original Greek word) is something God gives to those who believe God.
   - v 4: Justification isn't the result of works—it's not wages, because it's something credited i.e. a gift.
   - v 5: A saved person does not work. The saved person no longer trusts in obedience as the way to be saved. Instead, they trust God, who justifies the wicked, knowing that God has a way to save which is nothing to do with our efforts.

   NOTE: Paul's argument in verses 2-3 is: If Abraham's faith was simply his obedience/works, he had something to be proud of, and to offer (boast about). But this is impossible when we consider what we can offer God (end of verse 2). The conclusion shows that the idea of faith = obedience must be wrong. And Scripture proves Paul's argument (v 3): all Abraham did was that he "believed God."

   - **Read Genesis 15:1-6. How does this help us see what "faith" is?**
   Abram is childless (v 2-3). Further, his wife Sarai is barren (11:29-30). But God promises that he will have a son (15:4); and countless descendants (v 5). This is the promise, which humanly speaking is impossible, that Abram "believed" (v 6). Faith is trusting God's promises, even when they appear impossible; it is to hope in God to do what we know would, without him, have no hope of happening. (Questions 7 and 10 return to this theme.)

3. **Next, Paul looks back to David, the greatest king of Israel. What did David discover about forgiveness (v 6-8)?**
   "The same thing" as Abraham (v 6). It is blessed to have your transgressions (conscious sins) forgiven, to have your sins "covered" (v 7). This is possible for the man whose sin God doesn't reckon ("count") against him (v 8). So saving faith is trusting God both to not count our sin against us, and to count us right with him.

   ○ *OPTIONAL: From your knowledge of David's life, why would knowing that forgiveness is through faith, not works, have been precious to him?*
   2 Samuel 11: David (while a great, godly king of Israel) was an adulterer who conspired to murder an honorable man. The only righteousness he could have was one which was "apart from works" (Romans 4:6).

Explore More

- **What does this justified-by-faith person do (v 5, 8, 11)?**
  - *v 5: Confesses sin, rather than trying to cover it up (hiding it, excusing it, making up for it). Knowing we are justified by faith enables us to be honest about our sins.*
  - *v 8: Instructs and teaches others about God, and about forgiveness, and about living in response to forgiveness.*
  - *v 11: Rejoices in the Lord.*

- **Rewrite verses 1-2 and 7 as though David believed he was justified by his works, not his faith.**

  For example: "Blessed is he whose transgressions are outweighed by his good works, who has made up for his sins. Blessed is the man who has made himself acceptable to God and in whose spirit is no deceit. I am my own security; I protect myself from trouble and, having rescued myself, deserve to say that I have earned deliverance."

4. **How would you use verse 5 to explain to someone what saving faith isn't, and is?**

    Saving faith is not obedience. You cannot work and trust. Saving faith isn't, itself, righteousness. Faith is not a work that earns righteousness; it is an attitude which receives the gift of righteousness. Saving faith is humble; it acknowledges that, before God, we are "wicked" and need God to justify us, because we cannot justify ourselves. Saving faith is hopeful; it is a trust transfer, where we remove our hopes from our own efforts (or anything else), and place them on God as Savior, knowing that he gives right standing with him to those who trust him in this way.

5. **How is saving faith different from what many churchgoers or religious people think faith is?**
    - *Faith is not believing in God.* You can have lots and lots of strong faith that God exists, that he is loving, that he is holy. You can believe that the Bible is God's holy word. You can show great reverence for God. Yet all the while you can be seeking to be your own savior and justifier by trusting in your own performance in religion, in moral character, in vocation, in parenting, etc.
    - *Faith is not understanding that God saves, intellectually.* It is about trusting. I can know that a bridge will take my weight; but to cross it, I must trust that the bridge will take my weight, by stepping onto it.
    - *Faith itself does not save us; it is the object of the faith (God) who saves.* We do not deserve to go to heaven because we have put our trust in God; trust is not a work which earns righteousness. Rather, God graciously "credits" faith as righteousness. If we rely on our faith to save us, we'll grow anxious if we think we have less faith than we did, and have little assurance. If we rely

on God to save us, we'll enjoy complete assurance.
- NOTE: The Getting Personal section after question 5 picks up on this idea of what we are really trusting in to save us.

6. Why does the order in which these things happened in history matter for how we become righteous?

If God told Abraham to get circumcised, or if he gave his people the law, before he reckoned faith as righteousness, then it could be that faith = trust + circumcision, or = obedience to God's word. But Abraham was saved before circumcision, and well before the formal law was given by Moses. He was saved through trust in the promises of God. This matters for Jews (they need to rely on God's promises), and for Gentiles. Gentiles aren't Jews—they are uncircumcised and not necessarily brought up with God's law—but they are saved the same way: through saving faith.

- **What is Paul's conclusion (v 16-17a)?**
Everyone is saved as Abraham was, because the promise (i.e. benefitting from God's promise to bless us) "comes by faith." Abraham is the "father" not only of Israel (the Jews) but of "many nations"—of anyone who has the faith he did, no matter what their ethnicity or background.

7. What do we learn about believing God (i.e. having saving faith) in verses 18-22?

To "believe God" is to look at what God has said and to let that define reality for you. These verses show us how to do this:
- v 18-19: *Not to go on feelings or appearances.* Abraham hoped "against all hope" (v 18); "he faced the fact that his body was as good as dead" (v 19). He looked at his body and it looked hopeless; but he looked at God and believed. Faith is not optimism about life or faith in one's own abilities; it is going on trust in God despite our weaknesses or perceptions.
- v 20: *Give glory to God in anticipation of his promises coming true.* Abraham "gave glory to God" by living in trust, even though God's promise of a child had not yet been fulfilled.
- v 21: *Focus on facts about God.* Abraham was "fully persuaded that God had power." Faith is not an absence of thinking; it is thinking about reality in terms of who God is, rather than just reacting to circumstances. Abraham knew God had power. (He had created everything, which shows us God's divine power, Romans 1:20.) So, focusing on the facts he knew about God, he believed that although he and Sarah were too old to have children, God's power was sufficient to keep his promise.

- **How did Abraham's life show that he knew the truth of the end of verse 17?**
God gives life to the dead—and

Abraham trusted God to do exactly that, bringing a living baby into the dead place of Sarah's barren womb. He told Abraham he would be the father of many nations, even though he was not a father to anyone—and Abraham trusted God to be able to "[call] things that are not as though they were." If you have time, turn to Genesis 21:1-7 and Exodus 1:1-7, where we see these promises coming to fulfillment.

8. What does saving faith look like for us today (v 23-25)?

Our faith is to be of the same "sort" as Abraham's (v 23-24a); but we believe in God's promises in Jesus. The object of our faith is Jesus, the Son of God and descendant of Abraham; we believe that he died and rose and so we are justified. Abrahamic faith is total trust in Jesus to save us.

○ **OPTIONAL: How does the gospel show us that the end of verse 17 is true?**

The resurrection is the most thrilling example of God being "the God who gives life to the dead." And him calling us, and treating us as righteous even while we are still sinners, and promising to make us totally pure, is the ultimate example of him "[calling] things that are not as though they were." You could read Ephesians 2:1-7, where Paul describes how God brought us to life when we were dead.

9. What difference does being justified by faith make?

For each, think about how this changes us today.

- **v 2-3**

  We don't boast in ourselves. Our righteousness is credited, not earned; knowing this means we give glory to God (see verse 20), and have a humility about ourselves and great hope in Christ.

- **v 6-8**

  We don't cower. We know we are sinful, but we also know our sins are covered. We are free to be honest about our sins, rather than seeking to cover them up, because we know God covers them for us. We are joyfully grateful.

- **v 16**

  We enjoy assurance. The promise of inheriting the earth (i.e. enjoying eternal life in a renewed world—you may need to explain this) is of grace, and relies on God's promise-keeping power, not our law-keeping performance. When we sin, we don't need to fear for our future.

- **v 18**

  Hope when there is no hope. We can face loss, disappointment, and grief without feeling we have no hope, because our life rests only on God's promises.

10. **Share examples, from your own lives or those of Christian friends, of when having faith has resulted in...**
 • **having hope in a hopeless situation.**
 • **doing something difficult in obedience to God.**
 Give people a couple of minutes to write down some examples before you ask them to share. Make sure stories are kept fairly brief!

11. **What is faith, and what good is faith?**
 This refers back to question 1. We have seen that real, saving faith is a total trust in God's promise, through Christ's death and resurrection, to forgive, bless, and justify his people. When we place this faith in God, he reckons it as righteousness—that is, the result of faith is God undeservedly giving us right standing with him.

5

Enjoying Justification
Romans 5

The Big Idea
Justification by faith brings peace with God, access to him, certainty we will live with him, and joy in suffering. Justification is secured by Jesus, our representative.

Summary
NOTE: This is a long and, at times, complex section. We will not be looking in depth at every verse, nor do we have time to draw every teaching of Paul from this passage.

In verses 1-11, Paul lists some of the benefits of justification. There is peace with God; friendship with God; and certainty that we will one day be in the presence of God. But justification also changes the way we suffer: we do so rejoicing, because suffering starts a chain reaction that leads to greater hope—the benefits of justification are not only not diminished by suffering, they are enlarged by it.

Verse 12 begins "Therefore." What links verses 1-11 with verses 12-21 is the question: *How can one man's actions, however good and noble, affect so many people in such a life-changing way?* Paul's answer is that God deals with humanity through a "federal head"—one man acts on behalf of, and represents, many others. We are all born in Adam's humanity, and so since he sinned, we sinned, and since that sin brought death, so we die (v 12-14). But then Paul says that just as all that is true of Adam is true of us, if we put our faith in Christ, then all that is true of him is true of us.

So through Jesus, we can have righteousness, justification, and eternal life (v 18-19, 21)—all the benefits that Paul listed in verses 1-11 are what Christ has earned and enjoys, and if he is our representative, then we can enjoy them too.

Optional Extra

Give the group a list of scenarios in which they face a problem or challenge (e.g. you have a flat tyre; you are cooking a meal for 25 people; you have a math test at work; you can't understand a part of Leviticus; you need help planting flowers; you need to make peace with a neighbor whose fence you damaged). For each, ask people to say if they would rather someone else did the job on their behalf, and who they would pick from the group (or your church membership) to do that.

This is to introduce the idea of being represented by another, who (we hope!) will do a better job than us. Ask: *What will happen for us if they do a good job of the task? What will happen if they prove to be no better (or worse) than we would have been?* You could use this activity when you reach question 8 or 11.

Guidance for Questions

1. **Why is it good to be justified by faith?**

   This is an opportunity for you to confirm that your group understand what justification and faith are (based on the previous two studies), as well as to discuss what the benefits of justification are. You may like to ask, *What are the present benefits of justification* (i.e. there is more to it than having eternal life beyond death)?

2. **What benefits of justification does Paul list in verses 1-2?**
   - Peace with God (v 1). The state of hostilities between God and us is over. It is objective; it isn't dependent on how I feel.
   - Access into grace in which we stand (v 2). We are given a favorable position from which to develop a personal relationship with God. We can go to him with our requests, problems, and failures, and he hears and relates to us.
   - Hope of the glory of God (v 2). Hope = certain anticipation. (Unlike the way we usually use "hope", e.g. "I hope it will be sunny tomorrow.") Justification means we know for sure that we will be with God, sharing his glory, enjoying his presence.

○ **OPTIONAL: How is this more than being at peace with God?**
   Peace is merely the end of hostility. This is friendship.

3. **Imagine someone says, "That's lovely for you—but not for me, because my life is so full of suffering." What does Paul say about the difference being justified makes when we suffer (v 3-5, 11)?**
   "We also rejoice in our sufferings" (v 3); "we also rejoice in God through our Lord Jesus Christ" (v 11). When we suffer, we still know joy, because

"we know" that for the person who is justified by faith, suffering produces…
- *perseverance*, i.e. single-mindedness. Suffering helps us focus on what is really important, reminds us of what is lasting and what is not, and helps us to realign our priorities.
- *character*, i.e. testedness. This is the quality of confidence that comes from having been through an experience. If suffering leads you to focus on God and eternal things, then it will lead to greater confidence as you come through it.
- *growth in hope*, i.e. a stronger assurance of one's peace, access to God, and future glory.

- **Why does justification make this difference, do you think?**

Because if we are justified, we know that God loves us, that we are at peace with him, and that we are heading for glory in his presence. Justification means that we have God, and we rejoice in that relationship (v 11). This means that Christian joy does not depend on circumstances, and so it continues even in very hard times. If we seek our ultimate joy in our career, or relationships, or possessions, then if we lose them or they don't deliver joy, we will either be disappointed, or we will become detached, thinking joy is impossible for us. But if we are justified, our ultimate joy is in knowing God—and he does not change. We cannot lose him.

4. **In what two ways can we know that God loves us (v 5-8)?**
- First, verse 5: Because we experience his love. "God has poured out his love into our hearts," through the Holy Spirit. So every Christian has some inner, subjective experience of God's love. It can be quite a strong experience, though it can be mild and gentle too (which is more common).
- Second, verses 6-8: Because of the death of Jesus. Paul's point here is that it would take a very loving person to die for another, and even a very loving person would not die for an evil person; but that is what Jesus Christ did. While we were still rebelling against and resisting him, he died for us. This is an objective proof of God's love for us. While you were a sinner, God sent his own Son to die for you; therefore, whether you feel that he does or not, God loves you.

5. **What difference would it make if verse 3 said…**
- **rejoice about our suffering?**

This would be masochism: enjoying the fact that suffering has come. It actually is possible to rejoice about suffering. Some people need to feel punished in order to deal with their sense of guilt; others like to suffer because then they can feel superior toward people who have had an easier life.

- **rejoice beyond suffering?**

This would be stoicism: gritting your teeth and getting through it, because better times will come, and then you will know joy. Of course, the Christian knows that one day they will enjoy a life without any suffering; but they can know joy in suffering, because they find their joy in knowing God.

- **rejoice despite our suffering?**
We do rejoice despite our suffering; but verse 3 teaches us that we can do more than that. We don't need to try to ignore our suffering, and say, *I hate the suffering but at least I've got God*. Verse 3 says that suffering has a purpose; it is producing single-mindedness, and testedness, and greater hope. So Christians rejoice in suffering.

6. **How does suffering show where our hopes and dreams are really based?**
If suffering takes away our joy, it shows that we were locating our joy in the thing we have lost. If suffering makes us feel hopeless, then we were placing our hope in the thing we have lost, or are struggling with. For instance, if we lose our health, or our looks, and this makes us overwhelmingly sad or angry, then really our joy was not in knowing God, but in looking good or feeling fit. Or, if we are out of work for a long period, and feel that there's no point to life anymore, then we were finding our hope in our career. But if when hard times come, our hope grows, and our joy increases as we focus on knowing God now, and heading for our future with him, then this shows that we truly are someone who "rejoice[s] in God through our Lord Jesus Christ" (v 11).

7. **What do we need to remember when we suffer, and remind other Christians about when they suffer?**
That, if we keep a clear grasp of the truth that we are justified through grace, our suffering will produce more focus on what we have in Christ, will strengthen our character, and will enable us to know our hope more clearly. Suffering is not a disaster, it cannot remove what we most need, and it is not something to get through by gritting our teeth. It is something we can rejoice in.

NOTE: The Getting Personal section after question 7 is probably best read during the session and then reflected on at home, after the study.

8. **How did sin and death enter the world, and who do they affect (v 12-14)?**
Sin entered the world through one man (Adam); and so death entered the world, because it is the penalty for sin. And death affects all men, "because all sinned" (v 12). (There is no need to think at this point about what "all sinned" means—see the note in the Study Guide, p. 34, about how humans are represented either by Adam or by Jesus.)

NOTE: Verse 12 begins "therefore"; verses 12-21 are linked to the previous section. In light of all the benefits of justification in verses 1-11, Paul probably is anticipating the question: *How can one person's sacrifice (as noble as it was) bring about such incredible benefits to so many?* So Paul is now turning to show how Jesus' sacrifice benefits us—it is, as we'll see, because he was acting as our representative, just as Adam did.

- **How did grace enter the world (v 15)?**
  "By the grace of the one man, Jesus Christ." So sin and death entered through Adam; grace and life through Jesus.

9. **How are Adam and Jesus different, in what they did and in the effects their actions had (v 15-17)?**
    - v 15: Adam's action ("the trespass") brought death; Jesus' action ("the gift") brought grace. The salvation Jesus brought is more powerful than the sin Adam brought.
    - v 16: Adam's single sin (in the Garden of Eden; see Genesis 3:1-8) brought judgment and condemnation; Jesus' single "gift" offered justification for all sinners—won forgiveness for "many trespasses." Christ is able to cover not just Adam's sin but the sins of all those who trust him too.
    - v 17: Through Adam, death reigns; through Christ, people reign, in life.
    NOTE: These are complicated verses. The basic teaching to grasp is that Adam's sin brought death, whereas Christ's gift brought life; and that Christ's action is greater and more powerful than Adam's, and is able to cover all sin.

- **How are they similar (v 18)?**
  In being representatives. Adam's disobedience brought us guilt; Christ's obedience brings us righteousness/justification (v 18).

10. **How does verse 19 sum up what Paul has said in verses 12-18?**
    Before we acted, Adam's disobedience made us legally sinners, guilty. He represented us, so we sinned in him (v 12) and we are guilty in him. But before we acted, Jesus' obedience made us legally righteous (if we have him as our representative, rather than Adam).

- **Why does "the obedience of the one man," Jesus, matter to us?**
  Because his perfect obedience, in his life and his death, means that he is the only one who can be a representative who brings righteousness and life to us, rather than sin and death. Jesus obeyed for us, on our behalf; and God treats us according to Jesus' obedience. So Christ's obedience is a matter of life and death to us, because that obedience is our obedience if we have put our faith in Christ (i.e. if we have taken him as our representative, instead of Adam).

11. **Why is it good news that God deals with us through a representative?**
    Instinctively, we may feel that we don't want someone else to represent us. But if we each had to represent ourselves as individuals before God's heavenly throne, we would have no defense to make. (See 3:19

and Study 3.) Our sin would lead us to death. Instead, we are represented by Adam—and so we are still treated as sinners, because he sinned. But since we are represented by someone, then if there were an obedient man, he could represent us; he could act on our behalf, and through him we could have life. So it is wonderful news that God deals with us through a representative, because in Jesus we find the man who can represent us obediently, and in whom we can have the justification that, left to ourselves or left in Adam, we could never have.

12. **How would you use Romans 5 to encourage or challenge…**
- **a Christian who is unsure they are really loved and saved by God?**
v 5-8: Point them to the ultimate, objective demonstration of God's love for them—that even though they are sinful, Christ came to die for them. And then point them to the work of the Spirit in their hearts—likely, there have been times they have experienced God's love, and a sense of certainty, and this is another assurance to them. Encourage them to believe and live out the benefits of justification: to enjoy being at peace with God, to speak to him as a friend, and to look forward to seeing him.

- **a Christian who is suffering greatly?**
v 3-4: Encourage them to see their sufferings as a time when they can grow in perseverance, character, and hope. Point them to the true, lasting source of joy—all they have in God, through the Lord Jesus Christ.

- **a non-believer who is worrying about dying?**
They are right to worry! You can encourage them that they are seeing the world as it really is; death comes to all men. Explain why: because we are part of sinful humanity, born into sin, and facing death. Then point to the new humanity, headed by Jesus, who obeyed on our behalf and died for our sins, so that we can be part of his people, enjoying right standing with God and life with him. If they put their faith in him, God will count Jesus' obedience to them, and they won't need to worry about death anymore.

- **a non-believer who says: "I'm okay. I'm not a bad person"?**
The challenge from verses 12-21 is that, ultimately, all that matters is whether we are "in Adam" or "in Christ." If we are not in Christ, we are not okay—because we are part of sinful humanity, represented by sinful Adam, and so we face death and condemnation. The only way to be "okay" is to ask Christ to be our representative, so that God treats us as perfectly obedient, rather than sinners. We may self-identify as "not bad," but if we are in Adam, as humanity naturally is, then we are sinful, and facing death.

6

Why Christians Obey God

Romans 6:1 – 7:6

The Big Idea
We obey God because we know who we are: united with Christ, slaves of God, and married to Jesus.

Summary
From Romans 6:1 to 7:25, Paul is answering four questions (6:1, 15; 7:7, 13). The first two, which are covered in this study, are to do with why Christians obey God, since we are saved only by grace and not by anything we do.

In one sense, Paul's answer is not a detour. Paul will answer by re-explaining and applying the doctrine of justification by faith through union with Christ. The whole motivation for the Christian to obey God flows out of who we are—our new identity, which comes because we have died with Christ (6:3-4).

Yet in another sense, this does introduce a new section. The first five chapters of Romans explain what God has accomplished for us in the gospel; chapters 6 – 7, along with chapter 8 (which is covered in the second Good Book Guide to Romans), tell us what God will accomplish in us through the gospel. They tell us how the gospel is dynamite that produces massive changes in our thoughts and behavior, because it fundamentally changes who we are.

Optional Extra
Ask each group member to write down in three short sentences a description of who they are. Then ask what difference those descriptors make to how they think and feel and act. You could link back to this idea of our sense of identity shaping our lives and actions after questions 4 or 5, or at the end of the study.

Guidance for Questions

1. Christians are saved by grace, and not by works—so why bother obeying God or living a good life?

This is, in some ways, a very good question to ask about the gospel of "received righteousness." Since our moral efforts cannot contribute one bit to our salvation, why be good at all? Doesn't it give us license to keep on sinning, knowing we are forgiven, knowing there is always more grace for us?

Many Christians are unsure on how to answer this; others will give answers which are not the way Paul chooses to answer in this passage. Having discussed answers for a while, encourage your group to be ready to listen to the way Paul answers it in this passage.

You could return to this discussion after question 11, to see what people have added to their understanding.

2. **What answer, and what reason, does Paul give in verse 2?**
Absolutely not! You died to sin, so how can you carry on living in it?

3. **How does Paul explain what he means by "[you] died to sin"?**
- v 3-5
  - v 3: When Christians were baptized—by which Paul means, when they believed—they were united with Christ in his death (v 3). When he died, we died. Since Christ died, and his death achieved freedom from sin (Hebrews 2:14-15), and we died with him, we're therefore freed from sin.
  - v 4-5: Since Christ's death led to his resurrection and new life, in the same way our union with Christ will, and must, lead to a new life. If we believe in Christ, a change of identity has happened, so a change of life will happen.

- v 5-7
  Our "old self" has been killed, so that the "body of sin might be done away with." The "body of sin" is sin expressing itself through our bodies. Our "old self" is our pre-believing state and identity; and it has died, gone. The old me, in which sin controlled my personality and my life, died with Christ. So while a Christian can still sin, a Christian has died to sin in the sense that we are no longer under its power.

NOTE: Beware of the following wrong or inadequate views of what "died to sin" means, so that you can steer your group away from them if you need to:
- *We no longer want to sin, and sin has no more influence over us.* If this were the true meaning, Paul would not have had to urge us not to sin in verses 12-14.
- *We no longer ought to sin; it is inappropriate.* This is true, but doesn't go far enough. Paul doesn't say "you ought to die to sin" but "[you] died to sin."
- *We are slowly moving away from sin, and as it weakens, it dies.* But Paul's words have the sense of a finished, past, single action. Sin is not dying; it is dead.
- *We have decided to turn away from sin.* This is true, but not what Paul is saying here; sin died because Christ died, not because we did something. This "sin-death" is not the result of our determination to kill it, but because Jesus has died for us.

4. **Because Christians "died with Christ," what do we now know (v 8-10)?**
We will live with him (v 8). Since all that is true of Christ is true of us, we know that…
- he was raised, so we have been spiritually, and will be physically, raised.
- he cannot die again, since death has no hold over him, so we

cannot die again either (death here meaning the death of judgment and eternal punishment, rather than physical decay).
- he lives for God, so we will and should as well.

Explore More

○ **What do these passages teach us about what we have "in Christ"—that is, because we are united with him?**
There are many truths about the blessings we have from our union with Christ here—any time Paul says "in Christ / in him / with him," he's pointing us to a blessing. Don't get sidetracked by particular blessings—simply appreciate the sheer breadth and scale of what union with Christ brings the believer:
- 1:3: every spiritual blessing (Paul will go on to detail some of them…)
- 1:4, 11: chosen by God
- 1:5: adopted by God
- 1:6: received grace from God
- 1:12: able to praise God and live for him
- 1:13: given the Holy Spirit. Note that verse 13 tells us how to be "in Christ"—by hearing and believing the gospel.
- 2:5: made alive when we were dead and under God's wrath (v 1, 3)
- 2:6: raised and seated in heaven
- 2:7: shown and experiencing God's kindness now, as a foretaste of what we will enjoy in the future (the "coming ages")

○ **What should our response be (1:3, 6, 12, 14)?**
Praise. If we understand all we have through union with Christ by faith, we will respond by praising and living for God (v 12).

5. **What is the application Paul draws in verses 11-14 for anyone who died with Christ…**
- **negatively?**
See yourself as dead to sin (v 11); so do not let sin "reign" i.e. control any part of you, by obeying its evil desires (v 12). Sin is not to be our master (v 14).

- **positively?**
Think of yourself as alive to God—i.e. living in a way which obeys and pleases and enjoys knowing God (v 1). Proactively offer all you have to God (v 13). Let grace dominate and control you (v 14).

Encourage your group to think of ways they need to stop offering thoughts or actions or specific parts of their body to the control of their sinful desires; and ways they need to proactively and consciously use their thoughts, actions or body parts to obey God. Point out that when we are tempted to sin, we are not only to not follow our sinful desires, we are also to live for God in that moment.

6. **"If I fall into sin, it is because I do not realize who I am in Christ." How is this a good summary of Paul's message here?**

When we sin, we are going against our identity as people who have been raised to new life when Jesus was. We are living as though we had not died with Jesus, as though we are still the people we were before we believed.

7. **Who or what are we free to choose to serve (v 16-18, 22)?**

Either sin or obedience (v 16) / righteousness (v 17) / God (v 22).

○ *OPTIONAL: What point is Paul making about human freedom?*

No one is free—everyone is a slave to something or someone! We all live for something, and "offer" ourselves to that thing, serving it and living for it. (As Paul pointed out in 1:18-32, we either serve the Creator, or something created.) The thing we choose to serve becomes a master, and we its slaves. And ultimately, there are only two masters: God or sin.

8. **How does Paul compare and contrast these two masters?**
 * **v 19**

 Slavery to sin results in deterioration—the wickedness is "ever-increasing." As we act out of a particular purpose, that action shapes our character and will so that it becomes easier to act in that way again. Offering ourselves to sin leads to impurity, and ever greater sin. Slavery to God works in the same way—our character and will are shaped into habits of righteousness and greater and greater holiness.

 * **v 21-22**

 Slavery to sin results in death: ultimately, eternal condemnation and separation from God. But Paul here is talking of a "death" these Christians experienced before they believed. He is referring to brokenness of life—the "death" of enslavement to something other than God, which cannot deliver satisfaction or security. Paul is saying that the only benefit of serving sin is brokenness.

 So the results of slavery to God are a complete contrast—holiness in life now and eternal life to come.

 * **v 23**

 Sin gives us what we deserve—a wage, which is death. God gives us what we don't deserve—a gift, which is eternal life. Our serving God doesn't mean we deserve life from him. It is because he has given us the gift of life that we serve him.

○ *OPTIONAL: Someone says, "I don't want to be a Christian because I don't want to give up my freedom." What does verse 20 say about that "freedom"?*

If you don't put your faith in Christ and so begin to serve God, you are free but only from righteousness. The only freedom the non-Christian has is the freedom not to be right with God, and not to enjoy living in the way that is right for them. This is hardly a freedom worth having or keeping.

9. **How does this help us to answer these views?**

   (If you have little time, you could divide your group into four, taking one question each; or choose to focus on one or two of these.)

   - **"I just couldn't help sinning in that way."**

     If a non-Christian says this, in a sense they are right. Sin is their master; they are under its power. But if a Christian says this, they have forgotten who they are. A Christian never needs to sin, because we have been set free from the rule and mastery of sin. We can still sin; but we never have to sin.

   - **"I'm determined not to sin. I think to myself, 'Just say no!'"**

     The motive not to sin here is not the one that Paul gives us. We are not supposed to grit our teeth through life, trying to avoid sin (this doesn't work). We are to remember who we are in Christ—that our old, sinful self has died, and there is a new "me." Why would we want to sin? We can now live for God instead, in line with our new identity. That's the motivation for not sinning.

   - **"I find myself envying the freedom of my non-Christian friends."**

     They are not free—they are slaves to something, and they serve it, and it will deliver only brokenness and condemnation. The only thing they are free from is being righteous.

   - **"God is working in me to change me, so I just let him get on with it."**

     The Bible never tells us we do not need to make an active effort to act out, or live by, what we know is true of us. We deliberately have to offer ourselves to living in accordance with what the Bible tells us. We need to be (in how we live) who we already are (in Christ). We work hard to live his way, knowing he is working in us. (See Philippians 2:12-13.)

10. **What does this image teach us about…**

    - **a believer's relationship to the law?**

      We are released from it—i.e. from being motivated to obey it in order to be saved by it—in the same way as the death of a marriage partner ends that relationship. The law only binds those who are alive, and we died, when Jesus did. While in the marriage's case, it is the husband's death that allows the wife to be free to remarry, in our case it is our death which leaves us free from the law.

    - **a believer's relationship to the Lord Jesus?**

      Now, we "belong to" Christ (v 4). The whole purpose of ending our "marriage" to the law, through our death in him, was so "that you might belong to another." Becoming a Christian is a complete change in relationship and allegiance—we are married to Christ! To be a Christian is to fall in love with Jesus and to enter into a legal yet personal relationship as comprehensive as marriage.

11. **In what ways does getting married mean being less free? But why is a good marriage still a joy?**

   When you get married, you cannot simply live as you choose. You have a duty to consider your spouse. Equally, you cannot enter into another relationship as though you were not married; you are bound to one person, your spouse.

   But on the other hand, there is now the possibility of an experience of love, intimacy, acceptance, and security that you could not have if you stayed single. Because of this, giving up your freedom is a joy, not a burden. Assuming you are in a good marriage, you now get pleasure from giving pleasure to your spouse. You don't have to treat them well and do things for them, but you do anyway, because you want to.

   - **So how are these verses a great motivation to live Jesus' way?**

   This is Paul's ultimate answer to why Christians obey God. It pleases Jesus. We are not married to the law, having to obey it in order to be saved; we are married to Christ, loving to obey the law in order to please him. We don't have to obey Christ, but we want to, because we love him. Obedience becomes a joy, not a burden.

   ○ *OPTIONAL: How does the marriage image help us to understand what it means to serve "in the new way of the Spirit" rather than in "the old way of the written code" (v 6)?*

   It does not mean that the written law of God in the Scriptures has been left behind—that we don't need to know it or live obediently to it. Rather, it is our motivation that has changed. We don't obey the law to be saved by it, but because the Spirit assures us that, in Christ, we belong to him and are loved by God, and so we obey it out of love for our husband. The law is no longer our lord. Christ is.

12. **"Since we are saved by grace, why bother obeying God?" How would you answer this question based on the following verses?**

   - **6:1-14**

   Because we have died to sin, when we died with Jesus. We are new people, able to live a new life, so why would we want to go back to our old lives and sin?

   - **6:15-23**

   Because you are either a slave to God, or to sin. Living as a slave to God leads to holiness and life; living as a slave to sin leads to brokenness and death. Why would you obey sin instead of obeying God?

   - **7:1-6**

   We have died with Christ, so we belong to him, and are married to him. So we will obey God in order to please him, out of love rather than fear.

7

Warfare Within

Romans 7:7-25

The Big Idea
The law exposes our sin, and sin exploits the law to provoke sin. As we experience the reality of sinning even though we don't want to, we are discouraged about ourselves but hopeful because of Christ's rescue.

Summary
In this section, Paul gives us a very honest insight into his conversion, and his Christian life. It is another complex section, though when read through as a whole, the overall messages are clear.

First, Paul deals with the question of whether the law (which we are bound to, which arouses sinful desires, and which therefore leads to death, v 4-6) is itself bad or sinful. His answer is that the law in itself is not ineffective or flawed; it was his sin that made the law ineffective. The law exposed his sin; and his sin exploited the law to cause him to sin—as he read: "Do not covet," he found himself coveting. His summary is: the law is good, but I am sinful.

Next, Paul moves on to ask if the law is a killer—and answers that, no, sin is the killer. But in answering this question, he takes us to his inner battle as a Christian, the battle between his true self, which loves God and wants to obey him, and his sinful self, which leads him to do what he does not want to do. His honesty is comforting for us as Christians.

We experience (or should experience) the same battle, and the same feeling of wretchedness when we do not obey despite our desire to obey—and we have the same hope as Paul in verses 24-25, that Christ will deliver us.

NOTE: There are two difficult questions about this section. First, who is Paul talking about in verses 7-12? In verse 9, he says, "I was alive apart from law." How could a Jew be "apart from law," and how could he be "alive" when Romans 1 – 3 has made clear that no one is right with God without the gospel. The answer is likely that Paul was "apart from law" in the sense of not truly understanding its requirements—he saw it as an external, behavioral code, rather than about his heart-attitudes too. So he was "alive" in his self-perception—he thought he was pleasing and acceptable to God, but he wasn't.

Second, is Paul talking about himself as a non-believer or a believer in verses 13-25? Plenty of thoughtful people have been on either side of this question. Some believe that a Christian could not say, "I am unspiritual, sold as a slave to sin" (v 14); and he admits he sins compulsively (v 15, 18). But the evidence that Paul is talking of his present Christian experience is stronger:

- There is a change in verb tenses—verses 7-13 are past tense; verse 14 onwards is in present tense.

- Verses 7-13 talk about sin "killing" him—verses 14-23 about an ongoing struggle within him.
- Paul delights in God's law (v 22); in 8:7, he will say that unbelievers cannot delight in God's law in their heart of hearts.
- Paul recognizes that he is a lost sinner (v 18); verses 7-13 show that unbelievers are unaware of being lost.
- Paul finds his hope in the rescue of Jesus, not in himself (v 24-25).

Guidance for Questions

1. **Have you ever done something that you had previously decided not to do? What caused you to do it? How did it make you feel?**

   This could be something serious (e.g. drive dangerously; snap at kids) or less serious (wear a particular item of clothing; use a phrase that irritates you). It is an introduction to the theme of the second half of Romans 7: that in the Christian life, we find ourselves (as Paul did) not doing what we want to—disobeying God where we had resolved to obey him.

2. **What does the law do (v 7)?**

   The main purpose of the law is to show us the character of sin. Paul would not have known what was sinful, except that he read the law. The law exposes our sin.

3. **What does sin do as we read the law (v 8-10)?**

   It uses the law to encourage sin. When the commandment of God comes to us, it actually aggravates and stirs sin up in our hearts. As we read the law, our sin grows. This is what Paul means by "apart from law, sin is dead" (v 8). Until the command against an evil thing comes to us, we may feel little urge to do it; but when we hear the command, our sin seizes the opportunity (v 8) and springs to life (v 9).

   An example: you may be walking on a path next to a wood without any intention of entering the wood. Then you see a sign saying, "Keep out of the wood" and suddenly you start to wonder what is in the wood, and want to go into the wood and have a look, and feel that people shouldn't forbid others to enter woods. The command to keep out has made you want to come in.

4. **Why would coveting (i.e. envy) have been the commandment that "killed" Paul, do you think? (Hint: Remember that pre-Christian Paul seems to have focused on keeping the law externally.)**

   Paul had been a Pharisee, thinking of sin only in terms of external actions. This made it far easier to think of yourself as an obedient, law-abiding person. So he could look at the Ten Commandments and tick them off in terms of external behavior ("I haven't worshiped an idol-statue; I haven't lied or stolen, etc.") But the commandment "Do not covet" has everything to do with inwards attitudes and heart issues, because it is to be discontent with what God has given you. You cannot turn that into an external rule!

- **What happened when Paul really thought about the command "Do not covet" (v 11)?**

    Sin sprang to life—by producing covetous desires (v 8)—and he realized he was a sinner. So reading the commandment, and understanding it, "put me to death" (v 11).

Explore More

○ ***Read Exodus 20:1-17. Taking commandments 2–9 in turn, what sinful, internal heart-motive lies beneath each wrong behavior God commands us to avoid?***

  2. *Don't make an image: not trusting God but seeking help elsewhere*
  3. *Don't misuse God's name: not honoring God as you should*
  4. *Keep the Sabbath: assuming you know better than God about work and rest*
  5. *Honor your parents: selfishness or ingratitude*
  6. *Don't murder: hating or being angry with someone*
  7. *Don't commit adultery: not believing that God's rules for marriage are always best*
  8. *Don't steal: not believing that what God has given you is enough*
  9. *Don't give false testimony: not having the same concern for truth that God has*

5. **Share examples from your own life when…**
- **reading God's law has exposed your sin.**
- **your sinfulness has exploited your reading of God's law to encourage you to sin.**

    (Give group members a little time to think about these two questions. It would be good for you to prepare your own answers beforehand, to share with the group.)

6. **What is the deepest, "true" Paul like?**

    Verse 22 is the place to begin answering this question: "In my inner being I delight in God's law." This is like saying "my heart of hearts" or "my true self." Paul is recognizing that we are all aware of conflicting desires—that we have, in some sense, multiple selves. The true Paul delights in God's law and wants to obey it (v 15, 18b). His truest self—the one which ultimately controls his outlook and attitudes—is the one which loves God, and longs to follow his law.

- **So why is there a struggle?**

    Because even as a Christian, we still have a sinful nature within (v 18). It is part of Paul's nature that does what he hates (v 15). So he cannot keep the law, even though he wants to. In himself, he is unable to live as he should, and as he desires to. There is an ongoing conflict between the new, true Paul, who loves God, and the old, sinful Paul, who is a rebel against him.

NOTE: It may help to realize that Paul is using the word "law" in three different ways:
- Sometimes "law" means the law of God (as in v 14, 16, 22, 25).
- In verse 21, Paul uses the word "law" to denote a principle: "I find this law at work." Paul means: *I find this to be a general principle—the more I try to do good, the more evil comes at me.*
- In verses 23 and 25, Paul uses the word "law" to mean a force or power. "But I see another law at work in [my] members ... the law of sin." Paul is saying, *In my heart of hearts—my inner being (v 22), my mind (v 23)—I delight in God's law. God's law is now the main power in my heart and mind. But there is another power within me—the power of sin. It is not the ruling influence of my heart, but it is still within me and makes war against my deepest desires for holiness.*

7. What does Paul conclude about himself (v 24)?
"What a wretched man I am!"

- **Do you think this is a fair self-assessment? Why or why not?**
It is, though it is uncomfortable for us, since if the apostle Paul felt himself wretched when he looked at his thoughts and actions, then we must too. But Paul is correct in his view. He knows what is right, what pleases God; he longs to do it; and yet he does what is wrong. He knows what sin is, and who it offends; but he still sins.

8. How can Paul be wretched but not hopeless (v 24-25)?
Because, though in himself Paul is hopeless, he can look away from himself and his body's sinfulness, to what God has done through Jesus Christ. Paul cannot save himself, but he doesn't need to—Jesus has died, and will return to deliver the Christian.

9. How does Paul's experience as a Christian both warn and comfort us?
- No one ever gets so advanced in the Christian life that they no longer see their sin. The warning is that if we ever perceive ourselves to be "over" sin, then we are deceived.
- No one gets so advanced that they don't struggle with sin. It is very important to expect a fight with our sinful nature. In fact, these verses suggest that the more we progress in holiness, the more our sinful nature will fight.
- It is, though, very comforting when we struggle, to know that this is consistent with growing as a Christian. Conflict with sin, and even some relapses into sin, are the experience of being a Christian. When we struggle, this is not evidence that we are not Christian; when we feel wretched about our inability to obey God, it is not a certain sign that we are not saved.
- Verses 24-25 take us to the greatest comfort. Christ has died for our failings. And one day, Christ

will finally rescue us from our struggle with sin, and we will live in his kingdom, in perfect obedience. Our sin does not have the last word; Jesus does.

10. **How is this a good summary of Paul's attitude?**

    Without accepting the truth that we are wretched—that we are sinners who know and desire what is right and yet still do what is wrong—we will never grasp the glory of the gospel. Only as our hearts truly cry at our vileness will we really understand what it means to say, "Who will rescue me … ? Thanks be to God—through Jesus Christ our Lord." So a sense of our own inability and a sense of gratitude at Christ's salvation grow hand in hand.

- **What prevents us from feeling "wretched" (v 24) about our own vileness?**

    Take suggestions from your group. Some possibilities:
    - We don't read and reflect on God's law, and so we don't know what sin is.
    - We forget the seriousness of sin; or, knowing its seriousness, we make excuses for ourselves ("I wouldn't have shouted at him if he hadn't been driving so badly").
    - Other Christians make excuses for us ("Well, everyone struggles with that sin" or "You are under a lot of pressure at the moment though, aren't you?").

11. **How would you use this passage to…**
    - **challenge a Christian who is complacent about their sin?**
      If Paul's conclusion about himself is verse 24a, then shouldn't ours be too?
    - **encourage a Christian who is burdened by their sin?**
      If you know you are wretched, then you are now able to understand and appreciate God's grace to you in Christ! You don't need to be burdened by your failure; Christ has died for it. And you can know the joy of knowing that you are a great sinner, but that Christ is a greater Savior.

Optional Extra

Read through the whole of Romans 1 – 7 again. It might be best for you to read it all, allowing the members of your group simply to listen and meditate on the wonderful gospel truths that you've studied during these seven studies on these chapters.

Bible-Study Guide to
Romans 8–16
by Timothy Keller

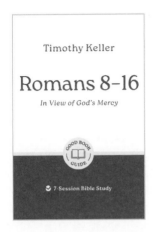

Continue in Romans with this seven-session Bible study by Timothy Keller, and see how Paul calls us to respond to God's amazing grace.

Each of the seven sessions has a simple, easy-to-follow structure with carefully crafted questions that help you look closely at the Bible text and apply it meaningfully to your everyday life. There is also a concise Leader's Guide at the back.

Explore the whole range of Good Book Guides

thegoodbook.com/gbgs
thegoodbook.co.uk/gbgs
thegoodbook.com.au/gbgs

BIBLICAL | RELEVANT | ACCESSIBLE

At The Good Book Company we are dedicated to helping Christians and local churches grow. We believe that God's growth process always starts with hearing clearly what he has said to us through his timeless and flawless word—the Bible.

Ever since we opened our doors in 1991, we have been striving to produce resources that are biblical, relevant, and accessible. By God's grace, we have grown to become an international publisher, encouraging ordinary Christians of every age and stage and every background and denomination to live for Christ day by day and equipping churches to grow in their knowledge of God, their love for one another, and the effectiveness of their outreach.

Call one of our friendly team for a discussion of your needs or visit one of our local websites for more information on the resources and services we provide.

Your friends at The Good Book Company

thegoodbook.com | thegoodbook.co.uk
thegoodbook.com.au | thegoodbook.co.nz